Cyber Confli
Essays from the Other Bank of the Rubicon

Cyber Conflict after Stuxnet: Essays from the Other Bank of the Rubicon

Hannah Pitts, *Editor*

A Cyber Conflict Studies Association publication
June 2016

CYBER CONFLICT AFTER STUXNET: ESSAYS FROM THE OTHER BANK OF THE
RUBICON
Copyright © 2016 by the Cyber Conflict Studies Assocation

Executive Editor: Hannah Pitts

Project Editor: Karl Grindal
Copy Editor: Emily Walz

ISBN-10: 0-9893274-4-2
ISBN-13: 978-0-9893274-4-2

LCCN: 2015951510

Contents

Foreign Reactions to Stuxnet

The World after Stuxnet

Index

Contributor Bios

Merritt Baer works in the Department of Homeland Security's Office of Cybersecurity & Communications. She works with both public and private sector entities to articulate and improve our federal civilian cybersecurity approach. Merritt has experience advising technology start-ups and all three branches of the US government. Merritt speaks regularly on emerging areas including the future of the Internet, current cybersecurity issues (cloud, mobile, IoT, and ICS), corporate interactions with government cyber, women in tech, entrepreneurship, and innovation. Her insights on business strategy and tech have been published in *Forbes*, *The Baltimore Sun*, Talking Points Memo, and ThinkProgress. Her academic work has been published by journals of Georgetown, Santa Clara, and the University of Virginia. Merritt is a graduate of Harvard College and Harvard Law School. She is admitted to the bars of New York, the US Court of Appeals for the Armed Forces, and the US Supreme Court. Based in Washington, D.C., she is a fellow at the EastWest Institute, an adjunct professor of cybersecurity at the University of Maryland, and an amateur boxer.

With engineering, economics, and comparative complex organization theory/political science degrees, **Dr. Chris C. Demchak** is a member of the Executive Board of the Cyber Conflict Studies Association (CCSA) and a senior professor with a named chair in cyber security and strategy, as well as a co-director of the Center for Cyber Conflict Studies (C3S), Strategic and Operational Research Department, US Naval War College. Her research and many publications address global cyberspace as a globally shared, complex, insecure "substrate" penetrating throughout the critical organizations of digitized societies, creating "cybered conflict," and resulting in a rising "Cyber Westphalia" of sovereign competitive complex socio-technical-economic systems (STESs). Demchak takes a systemic approach in focusing on emergent structures, comparative institutional evolution, adversary/defensive use of systemic cyber tools, virtual worlds/gaming for operationalized organizational learning, and designing systemic resilience against normal or adversary-imposed surprise. She has taught international security studies and management, comparative organization theory, enterprise information systems, and cybersecurity for international and national security issues. Recent works include *Designing Resilience* (2010, co-edited); *Wars of Disruption and Resilience* (2011); and a manuscript in production tentatively titled *Cyber Westphalia: Redrawing International Economics, Conflict, and Global Structure.*

Robert Fonow is a turnaround manager, management consultant, and educator based in Beijing and Northern Virginia, operating RGI Ltd., a Virginia corporation. Fonow's technology consulting concerns the development of the international telecommunications network and Internet. As an adjunct research fellow, he has written several articles for the National Defense University on vulnerabilities in the Internet. He served as the US State Department's senior consultant to the Iraqi government for ICT reconstruction in Iraq from 2006 to 2008, which remains a reconstruction success. Following Iraq, he participated in a USTDA data communications and Internet development project in the West Bank of Palestine from 2009 to 2013. Fonow has conducted commercial turnaround assignments in the United States, Britain, Switzerland, Russia, Japan, and China and was the first US State Department business delegate to the APEC Telecom

Working Group. He serves as the chairman of Discover Club, an after-school program in Haidian, the university area of Beijing. Further information is available on LinkedIn: Bob Fonow.

Dr. Catherine Lotrionte is the director of the CyberProject in the School of Foreign Service at Georgetown University, where she teaches and writes on international and national security law, international affairs, and technology. At Georgetown, she founded the CyberProject in 2008, focusing on the role of international and domestic law in recent and emerging developments in the proliferation of weapons, technology, and threats. In 2002, she was appointed by General Brent Scowcroft as counsel to the president's Foreign Intelligence Advisory Board at the White House, a position she held until 2006. In 2002, she served as a legal counsel for the Joint Inquiry Committee of the Senate Select Committee on Intelligence, investigating the September 11th terrorist attacks. Prior to that, Professor Lotrionte was assistant general counsel with the Office of General Counsel at the Central Intelligence Agency, where she provided legal advice relating to foreign intelligence and counterintelligence activities, international terrorism, espionage, and information warfare. Before working in the Office of General Counsel, she served in the US Department of Justice. She is an internationally recognized expert on international law and cyber conflict. Professor Lotrionte holds a PhD from Georgetown University and a JD from New York University and is the author of numerous publications, including two forthcoming books, *Cyber Policy: An Instrument of International Relations, Intelligence and National Power* and *U.S. National Security Law in the Post-Cold War Era*. She is a frequent speaker at cyber conferences across the globe and has founded and hosted for five years the annual International Conference on Cyber Engagement at Georgetown University. Dr. Lotrionte currently serves on the World Economic Forum's Global Agenda Council on Cybersecurity, the CSIS Cyber Task Force, the CFR Cyber Task Force, and the CFR Task Force on US Policy Toward North Korea. She is a life member of the Council on Foreign Relations.

Tim Maurer co-leads the Cyber Policy Initiative at the Carnegie Endowment for International Peace. His work focuses on cyberspace and international affairs, with a concentration on global cybersecurity norms, human rights online, and Internet governance. He serves as a member of the Research Advisory Network of the Global Commission on Internet Governance, the Freedom Online Coalition's cybersecurity working group "An Internet Free and Secure," and co-chaired the Civil Society Advisory Board of the Global Conference on CyberSpace. In 2014, he developed the Global Cyber Definitions Database for the chair of the OSCE to support the implementation of the OSCE's cyber confidence-building measures. His work has also been published by Jane's Intelligence Review, *Time, Foreign Policy*, CNN, Slate, and other academic and media venues. Prior to joining Carnegie, Maurer was the director of the Global Cybersecurity Norms and Resilience Project at New America and head of research of New America's Cybersecurity Initiative. He also gained experience with the United Nations in Rwanda, Geneva, and New York focusing on humanitarian assistance and the coordination of the UN system. He is a graduate of the Harvard Kennedy School with a Master in Public Policy.

Adam Segal is the Maurice R. Greenberg senior fellow for China studies and director of the Digital and Cyberspace Policy Program at the Council on Foreign Relations (CFR). An expert on security issues, technology development, and Chinese domestic and foreign policy, Segal was the project director for the CFR-sponsored Independent Task Force report Defending an Open, Global, Secure, and Resilient Internet. His book The Hacked World Order: How Nations Fight, Trade, Maneuver, and Manipulate in the Digital Age (PublicAffairs, 2016) describes the increasingly contentious geopolitics of cyberspace. His work has appeared in the Financial Times, The Economist, Foreign Policy, The Wall Street Journal, and Foreign Affairs, among others. He currently writes for the blog, "Net Politics."

Before coming to CFR, Segal was an arms control analyst for the China Project at the Union of Concerned Scientists. There, he wrote about missile defense, nuclear weapons, and Asian security issues. He has been a visiting scholar at the Hoover Institution at Stanford University, the Massachusetts Institute of Technology's Center for International Studies, the Shanghai Academy of Social Sciences, and Tsinghua University in Beijing. He has taught at Vassar College and Columbia University. Segal is the author of Advantage: How American Innovation Can Overcome the Asian Challenge (W.W. Norton, 2011) and Digital Dragon: High-Technology Enterprises in China (Cornell University Press, 2003), as well as several articles and book chapters on Chinese technology policy.

Segal has a BA and PhD in government from Cornell University, and an MA in international relations from the Fletcher School of Law and Diplomacy, Tufts University.

Ambassador J. Stapleton (Stape) Roy is a distinguished scholar and founding director emeritus of the Kissinger Institute on China and the United States at the Woodrow Wilson International Center for Scholars in Washington, D.C. Stape Roy was born in China and spent much of his youth there during the upheavals of World War II and the Communist Revolution, where he watched the battle for Shanghai from the roof of the Shanghai American School. He joined the US Foreign Service immediately after graduating from Princeton in 1956, retiring forty-five years later with the rank of career ambassador, the highest in the service. In 1978, he participated in the secret negotiations that led to the establishment of US-PRC diplomatic relations. During a career focused on East Asia and the Soviet Union, Stape's ambassadorial assignments included Singapore, China, andIndonesia. His final post with the State Department was as assistant secretary for intelligence and research. On retirement, he joined Kissinger Associates, Inc., a strategic consulting firm, before joining the Woodrow Wilson International Center for Scholars in September 2008 to head the newly-created Kissinger Institute. In 2001, he received Princeton University's Woodrow Wilson Award for Distinguished Public Service.

A research fellow with MIT Sloan School's Initiative on the Digital Economy, **Michael Schrage** has done unclassified advisory work on cyber conflict and national security issues for DARPA, the National Security Council, and the Office of Net Assessment. He has also published research on "complex systems procurement" with the Center for Strategic and International Studies (CSIS). His current academic research focuses on the design of "network effects" and "multiple selves" in human capital investment.

Peter Warren Singer is strategist and senior fellow at New America; a consultant for the US military, intelligence community, and industry; and a contributing editor at *Popular Science*. His books include *Cybersecurity and Cyberwar: What Everyone Needs to Know* and *Ghost Fleet: A Novel of the Next World War*. More at www. pwsinger.com.

Timothy L. Thomas is an analyst at the Foreign Military Studies Office (FMSO) at Fort Leavenworth, Kansas. He retired from the US Army as a Lieutenant Colonel in the summer of 1993. Mr. Thomas received a BS from West Point and an MA from the University of Southern California. He was a US Army Foreign Area Officer who specialized in Soviet/Russian studies. His military assignments included serving as the director of Soviet Studies at the United States Army Russian Institute (USARI) in Garmisch, Germany; as an inspector of Soviet tactical operations under CSCE; and as a Brigade S-2 and company commander in the 82nd Airborne Division. Mr. Thomas has done extensive research and publishing in the areas of peacekeeping, information war, psychological operations, low intensity conflict, and political-military affairs. He is the assistant editor of the journal *European Security*; an adjunct professor at the US Army's Eurasian Institute; an adjunct lecturer at the USAF Special Operations School; and a member of two Russian organizations, the Academy of International Information and the Academy of Natural Sciences.

Nader Uskowi is an expert on Iran and the Middle East with years of experience as an advisor and consultant on Iranian and regional affairs. Currently, he is the senior policy advisor with the United States Central Command (CENTCOM). Previously, he served as a senior political advisor with a Department of Defense task force in Afghanistan. He was also the founding editor of *Uskowi on Iran*. Nader is a graduate of the University of Southern California's School of International Relations and holds his MA degree from the George Washington University. He lives with his wife, Patti, in Reston, VA.

Foreword

With the discovery of Stuxnet in 2010, the cyber conflict community crossed a strategic Rubicon.[1] For years, Cassandras had warned of a future in which networked cyberspace would move beyond hacking and espionage to become a battlefield with effects in in the real world. Stuxnet proved this was possible. After careful testing, the Stuxnet malware found its way into closed industrial control system networks controlling Iran's nuclear centrifuges and subtly caused them to destroy themselves in a way that looked like random, unexplainable malfunctions.

The fact that Stuxnet attacked industrial control systems is important because these embedded networks increasingly run the world in which we live. While the malware was precisely designed to only target a specific centrifuge cascade with a specific configuration, an inert version of Stuxnet nonetheless escaped into the wild and was found in control systems all over the world. A less discriminating piece of software might have set off uncontrollable cascade effects, perhaps even boomeranging back on the designers.

As people analyze the implications of industrial control system hacking, it has become clear that the electric power grid is the most critical of the critical infrastructures. Indeed, all of the other critical infrastructures (water, banking, communications, transportation, gas, etc.) are completely dependent upon the underlying electrical layer. The first clues of the potentially devastating consequences of hacking against the grid and our lack of resiliency can be seen in the wake of the planet's increasingly unpredictable and severe weather events.

Hurricane Isabel in 2003 knocked out the power to Northern Virginia, which had the secondary effects of taking the two local water treatment plants offline, disrupting cellular communications, and causing widespread food spoilage. Within days, it seemed as though the social fabric itself was beginning to tear from the exposed lack of infrastructure resilience. Later disasters, such as Hurricanes Katrina and Sandy, only reinforced the conclusion that our current infrastructure is surprisingly fragile in the face of natural phenomena, and therefore highly vulnerable to malware that attacks industrial control systems.

This edited volume represents the first effort to comprehensively analyze Stuxnet and its implications. It brings together an interdisciplinary group of experts to examine the incident's strategic, legal, economic, military, and diplomatic consequences. The essays explore Stuxnet in the context of both international and US domestic law; reveal the varied reactions in Beijing, Moscow, and Tehran; and offer confidence-building measures and frameworks for dealing with a post-Stuxnet world.

"Cyber Conflict after Stuxnet: The View from the Other Bank of the Rubicon"
by Adam Segal

The Stuxnet Story

I N LATE 2009 OR EARLY 2010, Iran replaced about 1,000 IR-1 centrifuges of the 9,000 deployed at the Fuel Enrichment Plant (FEP) at Natanz. The natural assumption at the time would have been that the centrifuges had broken. Centrifuges are delicate machines spinning at incredibly high speeds, and Iran's IR-1 centrifuges were more temperamental than other designs, tending to break frequently. Still, the pace at which the centrifuges were breaking would have caused much chagrin for the Iranians and some head-scratching for outside observers.[2]

The operators of Natanz were right to be worried. The damaged centrifuges were the target of a sophisticated cyberattack, allegedly planned and launched by the United States and Israel in order to slow down Iran's nuclear program, code-named "Olympic Games." In 2005, Iran abandoned the Paris Agreement, under which Tehran agreed to a voluntary and temporary suspension of uranium enrichment. In April 2006, President Mahmoud Ahmadinejad announced that Iran had successfully enriched uranium. The program, and the number of centrifuges, grew over the next several years.

The United States and its European allies pursued sanctions through the United Nations. In July 2006, the United Nations Security Council demanded the complete suspension of enrichment and reprocessing-related activities, and, at the end of the year, levied sanctions on nuclear and missile technologies, though these were weakened by Russia and China. Resolutions in 2007 and 2008 expanded the sanction lists to additional individuals and entities.

While the failure of diplomatic efforts and the sanctions program inspired the White House to search for other tools to derail the Iranian program, the direct motivation for the cyberattacks apparently came in part from a request from Israel for bunker-busting bombs from the United States and for a request to fly over Iraq to reach Natanz in 2008. The Bush administration doubted that airstrikes would do much to set Iran's nuclear program back, and, already engaged in wars in Iraq and Afghanistan, feared an attack could ignite an even larger conflagration across the Middle East. President Bush denied the request but increased intelligence-sharing and briefed Israeli officials on new covert efforts to sabotage the Iranian nuclear program, including the cyber program.[3] When he came into office, President Obama continued and accelerated these covert efforts. The president reportedly told aides that if Olympic Games failed there would be no time for a new round of sanctions and diplomacy to work.[4]

Sometime in the summer of 2010, Stuxnet escaped into the wild. An Iranian engineer who had connected his computer to the centrifuges connected to the Internet. The malware would eventually spread to more than 115 countries. Chevron would be the first US company to acknowledge infection.[5] A little known Belarussian security firm, VirusBlokAda, was the first to identify Stuxnet and over the next year, researchers at Symantec, Kaspersky, and Langner Group worked to uncover the workings and purpose of the code. During this process, and in further investigations, these groups uncovered two other related malware programs—Flame and Duqu—that supported the Stuxnet attack through espionage.[6]

From a technical perspective, the attack inspired awe and admiration. One journalist called Stuxnet "probably the most interesting piece of malware I've ever covered."[7] To see why, it is useful to break the attack into three parts. First, there was preparation. Targets had to be identified and mapped. An electronic blueprint of the computers controlling the centrifuges at Natanz had to be created. Israel reportedly acquired and installed P-1 centrifuges, which were similar to Iran's, and then tested the malware on them at Dimona nuclear complex. The United States also acquired P-1s from Libya and tested them in national laboratories. The Department of Homeland Security and Idaho National Laboratory studied Siemens control systems in 2008.[8]

Second, there was the infiltration. Stuxnet had to enter a system that was not connected to the Internet: it had to jump the "air gap" though a thumb or other removable drive inserted by an engineer, maintenance worker, or supplier. When the thumb drive was inserted into a machine, the malware woke up, exploiting a vulnerability in Windows and dropping an encrypted file on the machine. It used two digital certificates stolen from Taiwanese companies to install fake drivers and infect machines and networks. The malware then looked for Siemens Step7 software, which is used to program industrial control systems that operate equipment such as centrifuges. Stuxnet moved next to undermine the programmable logic controllers.

The attack involved 5 zero-days, unknown vulnerabilities that have not been previously identified and so there have been zero days to patch. Zero-days are highly valued attack tools, often expensive and closely held. A normal attacker might use one, maybe two.

Finally, there was the execution. Stuxnet had a "dual warhead." One damaged centrifuges by speeding them up and slowing them down and opening and closing valves that connected six centrifuge cascades. The other masked the damage it was doing, sending fake reports back to operators. Stuxnet would also periodically connect to the Internet to update itself. Ralph Langner, a German cybersecurity expert who was among the first to decode bits of Stuxnet, estimated that 50 percent of the malware's development costs went into efforts to hide the attack. It also had a "kill switch" command embedded in the code, designed to prevent it from spreading and damaging other industrial control systems that did not match the precise configuration of the cascades at Natanz. On June 24, 2012, Stuxnet stopped functioning.

Once the operation and purpose of Stuxnet became public, there was (and continues to be) apprehension about future attacks; evaluation of the outcome; and speculation on what effect the digital weapon would have on international relations, governance of the Internet, and the future of cyber conflict. The ability of digital code to produce physical effect had long been predicted and had been produced under controlled circumstances.[9] With Stuxnet, it had happened "in the wild." A digital assault had taken control of an industrial control system and had been directed at a facility clearly identified as critical infrastructure. General Hayden, in the quote that gives this volume its name, called this "crossing the Rubicon," and there was a shared sense that Stuxnet opened the possibility of a new wave of attacks, many of them directed at the United States. "If you are in the glass house, you should not be the one initiating throwing rocks at each other," Gregory Rattray, former head of information security at JPMorgan, said at a 2012 conference. "We will have rocks come back at us."[10]

The fear of attack encompassed perceived threats not only from nations or state-backed attackers, but also from nonstate and criminal hacking groups. Parts of the Stuxnet code were shared on hacker forums, and there was a demonstration effect. "Regular cybercriminals look at something that Stuxnet is doing and say, that's a great idea, let's copy that," said Roel Schouwenberg, a researcher at Kaspersky.[11] Ralph Langner echoed the same threat: "Just by its media presence, Stuxnet and attacks against control systems will become irresistible for the hacker community. This is one thing that we have seen and that we will continue to see – these folks just out of curiosity and in the interest of getting media exposure, start playing around and [find] vulnerabilities."[12]

IMAGINING THE DECISIONMAKING PROCESS

Before evaluating the outcomes of the attack, the goals of the Stuxnet attack must be identified. From these goals, it is also possible to suggest the equities and interests involved in decisionmaking processes in the Bush and Obama administrations.

The first and most obvious goal was to slow and degrade the Iranian nuclear program. As former secretaries of state Henry Kissinger and George Schultz argue, "For 20 years, three presidents of both major parties proclaimed that an Iranian nuclear weapon was contrary to American and global interests—and that they were prepared to use force to prevent it."[13] There were clear national security and reputational risks to doing nothing.

Washington also had to respond to the concerns of its friends and allies in the region. After the 1981 strike on Iraq's Osirak reactor, Israel announced what became known as the Begin Doctrine: "On no account shall we permit an enemy to develop weapons of mass destruction against the people of Israel." At the time of Stuxnet's conception, Israel saw (and continues to see) the Iranian program as an existential threat. Shaul Mofaz, former Israel Defense Forces (IDF) chief of staff and then deputy prime minister, told an Israeli newspaper in 2008 that, "if Iran continues to develop nuclear weapons, we will attack it."[14] In addition, the memory of the Israeli air strike on Syria's nuclear reactor in September 2007 would have been fresh in the minds of all policymakers involved.

The Bush administration would have also heard calls for action from many of Iran's Arab neighbors. According to State Department cables published by Wikileaks, leaders of Egypt, Saudi Arabia, and the United Arab Emirates encouraged the United States to stop Iran's nuclear program. In 2006, for example, the United Arab Emirates' defense chief, Crown Prince Mohammed bin Zayed, told Commander of the United States Central Command General John Abizaid that the United States needed to take action against Iran "this year or next."[15]

The evidence of whether Stuxnet met its primary goal is mixed, though there seems to be a consensus that the attack slowed down work at Natanz by somewhere between eighteen and twenty-four months. Iran admitted it was a victim of cyberattacks but, not surprisingly, downplayed the impact. In a press conference, Iranian President Mahmoud Ahmadinejad said, "They succeeded in creating problems for a limited number of our centrifuges with the software they had installed in electronic parts."[16]

In a preliminary assessment, researchers at the Institute for Science and International Security concluded that if Stuxnet's goal "was to destroy a more limited number of centrifuges and set back Iran's progress in operating the FEP [fuel enrichment plant at Natanz] while making detection of the malware difficult, it may have succeeded, at

least for a while." A follow-up report found that while Iran worked
to maintain and accelerate the production of low-enriched uranium
during the time of the attacks, Stuxnet delayed Iran from expanding
the total number of enriching centrifuges and kept large sections of
the plant idle for many months. Iran may have also been reaching the
limits on raw materials needed to build IR-1s. Destroying a thousand
centrifuges would have significantly taxed the program, and may have
slowed the nuclear program long enough for Western sanctions to
have the desired effect of forcing Iran back to the negotiation table.[17]

There were other adverse effects. With the causes of the centrifuge damage unknown, Iranian operators would have lost confidence
in their production and quality control processes. As one official
told the New York Times, "The thinking was that the Iranians would
blame bad parts, or bad engineering, or just incompetence." The official continued, "The intent was that the failures should make them
feel they were stupid, which is what happened."[18] Once Stuxnet was
exposed, the Iranians would have had a high degree of uncertainty
about whether other computer systems were vulnerable or already
exploited.

While the public consensus is that the attack slowed Iran's progress, there are also doubters of the malware's efficacy. In a Royal
United Services Institute study, Ivanka Barzashka argues that if Stuxnet's purpose was "to decrease Iranian nuclear-weapons potential, it
clearly failed." As evidence, the total enrichment capacity of Natanz
grew in 2010 relative to previous years. Moreover, it is likely that Iran
accelerated and became more adept at hiding its nuclear program
after the attack.[19]

Given the objective of the attack as well as direct and indirect
political pressure to act, Washington would have weighed the idea of a
digital assault against alternate forms of sabotage and larger kinetic attacks, especially bombing or Special Forces attacks. Israeli intelligence
was apparently already killing Iranian scientists. In January 2010, a
remote-controlled bomb attached to a motorcycle killed Masoud
Alimohammadi, a physics professor, just as he stepped outside of his
home in the north of Tehran. These attacks had a limited effect and
there is no evidence the United States considered similar attacks.

The alternate scenario most discussed was airstrikes. Given Iranian efforts to hide the program at different sites throughout the country and to harden facilities, most thought a strike would only temporarily impede Iran's program and could lead to Iranian retaliation and possibly wider conflict. Defense Secretary Robert M. Gates reportedly convinced President Bush that an attack would not work and could lead to the expulsion of international inspectors, making Iran's nuclear efforts more opaque. Chief of Staff of the Israel Defense Forces Lieutenant General Gabi Ashkenazi also admitted that an aerial attack would only set back Iran's nuclear program two or three years. Israeli officials also expected that Hezbollah and Hamas, under the direction of Tehran, would retaliate, perhaps even in the United States.

According to David Sanger's account, President Bush turned to Condoleezza Rice and Stephen Hadley to develop a "third option" between bombing and doing nothing. Technical development occurred between a team established by then-Vice Chairman of the Joint Chiefs of Staff General James Cartwright and the National Security Agency (NSA). From the beginning, the Bush administration saw the need for Israeli participation. Unit 8200, Israel's cyber forces, had technical expertise that rivaled the NSA's, and Israeli intelligence had detailed knowledge of the Natanz facility.

The "third option" would have also had to be weighed against other US interests. Despite the immense efforts to keep the malware hidden, there would (or should) have been discussions about how long the United States could expect Stuxnet would remain invisible to the Iranians and the rest of the world. The inevitability of discovery should have been part of any decisionmaking calculus.

Although signed by President Obama in October 2012, well after Olympic Games was launched, Presidential Policy Directive 20 suggests some of the processes and internal debates that might have surrounded the attack on Natanz. Leaked by Edward Snowden, PPD-20 establishes "updated principles and processes as part of an overarching national cyber policy framework." PPD-20 calls on the National Security Staff to formalize a Cyber Operations Policy Working Group as the "primary forum" below the level of the Interagency Policy

Committee. The working group is not operational, but discusses issues that might arise during defensive and offensive cyber operations. The planning of operations is expected to involve "State, DOD, DOJ, DHS, members of the IC, and relevant sector specific agencies." Unresolved conflicts are to be raised to the Deputies and Principals Committees level.[20]

Under the heading of "offensive cyber effect operations" (OCEO), PPD-20 instructs the US government to "identify potential targets of national importance where OCEO can offer a favorable balance of effectiveness and risk as compared with other instruments of national power, [and] establish and maintain OCEO capabilities integrated as appropriate with other US offensive capabilities." It is also requires presidential authority for an attack that is likely to produce "significant consequences," defined as "Loss of life, significant responsive actions against the United States, significant damage to property, serious adverse US foreign policy consequences, or serious economic impact on the United States."[21]

Later in the document, PPD-20 lays out six criteria for policymaking: impact, risks, methods, geography and identity, transparency, and authorities and civil liberties. Again, it seems reasonable to assume that similar categories were used in Stuxnet decisionmaking. The potential risks are broadly defined, involving intelligence loss; retaliation or other impacts on US networks or interests (including economic); impact on the security and stability of the Internet; damage to foreign policies, bilateral and multilateral relationships, including Internet governance frameworks; and the establishment of unwelcome norms of international behavior. The category of methods focuses on intrusiveness, timeliness, efficiency, and capacity of the tools used.

While the six criteria seem fairly clear and straightforward, Stuxnet highlights how difficult applying them must be in practice. During the process, policymakers would have been aware that they were operating under a high degree of uncertainty about the future. They were entering a new world. There was also likely to be an implicit assumption that as digital assaults became more common, their impact would become easier to evaluate. Other cases would generate more data, which then could be fed back into the decisionmaking process.

Five years after the attack on Natanz became public, that assumption must be questioned. Some trends are clearer: Stuxnet, for example, has reinforced the trends of greater White House reliance on covert actions and the subsequent undermining of congressional oversight. But the impact on US strategic, diplomatic, and economic interests, as well as on the stability, security, and governance of the Internet, remains uncertain and contested.

Stuxnet and the Law

STUXNET AND US DOMESTIC LAW

Stuxnet presents new challenges to national security laws, both domestic and international. There are obvious definitional issues. In his contribution to this volume, Merritt Baer gives the example of the War Powers Resolution, which requires the president to consult with Congress "before introducing United States Armed Forces into hostilities."[22] But the definitions of "introducing forces" and "hostilities" are undetermined in a cyber context. Has an operator sitting at Fort Meade while moving remotely around Iranian networks been "introduced" to "hostilities"? Moreover, the president may use force for up to sixty days without involving Congress. Does that include the total time to prepare an attack, or just the duration of the attack itself?

There is also the related political question of appropriate authority: namely, under what authorities attacks can be ordered, and if cyberattacks prove especially difficult for Congress to oversee, whether they will result in a shift of power to the executive branch. Because US officials have not openly spoken of Olympic Games, there has been no public discussion of the authorities under which it was conducted. The attacks clearly fall under the definition of a covert operation: "activity or activities of the United States Government to influence political, economic, or military conditions abroad, where it is intended that the role of the United States Government will not be apparent or acknowledged publicly."[23] The Harvard Law School scholar Jack Goldsmith speculates that the operation might have occurred under the president's Article 2 powers. While these powers

13

have traditionally been limited to justifying the defense of US persons and property, they have also been invoked since the Korean War to support uses of force in defense of the integrity of the UN Charter.[24] In this framing, Iran's pursuit of a nuclear weapons program in contradiction to the Treaty on the Non-Proliferation of Nuclear Weapons and numerous UN resolutions would warrant cyberattacks in defense of the charter.[25]

According to Sanger, as the program shifted from the Bush to the Obama administration, there were members of the National Security Council who were uncomfortable with extending a covert program without a full review of its implications. In addition, the shift of responsibility for the program from the Pentagon to the intelligence community, done at the insistence of Secretary of Defense Robert Gates, meant the president had to review and renew the presidential findings that had allowed the attack to move forward. Sanger argues that members of the intelligence community were worried about the pause in operations that would have to occur if the old findings were redrawn. To avoid that problem, the Obama administration amended the Bush findings.

In his discussion of cyber offense and executive war-making authority, Eric Lorber argues that "neither the War Powers Resolution nor the Intelligence Authorization Act can effectively regulate most types of offensive cyber operations."[26] As noted above, the definition of introduction of armed forces is unlikely to apply in cyber operations. Code is not made up of US troops and so would not invoke the War Powers Resolution. In the case of the Intelligence Authorization Act, which requires the president to report covert actions to Congress, a cyberattack would fall under the extremely broad exception to the reporting requirement allowed for "traditional military activities." The president could invoke this exception on solid ground: many members of the NSA are dual-hatted to Cyber Command and so operations could be executed by military personnel; the president can launch cyber operations if they are in anticipation of hostilities; and any cyberattack could be considered part of operational planning.

Lorber concludes that cyberweapons add another component to the already-clear trend of increasing presidential reliance on covert action to avoid the requirements of the War Powers Resolution. Moreover, the secrecy surrounding cyber programs raises questions about the efficacy of congressional oversight and is likely to result in an increase in executive authority. Cyberattacks, in effect, give the president a new tool and greater flexibility.

STUXNET AND INTERNATIONAL LAW

US officials have consistently stated that they believe that cyberspace is not a "law-free zone," but one where international law applies. In 2012, for example, Harold Koh, then-legal advisor for the State Department, said in a speech at Cyber Command that while other countries question "whether existing bodies of international law apply to the cutting edge issues presented by the internet," the United States government has "made clear our view that established principles of international law do apply in cyberspace."[27] PPD-20 states that defensive and offensive cyber operations conducted under the directive must be "consistent with [the United States government's] obligations under international law, including with regard to matters of sovereignty and neutrality, and, as applicable, the law of armed conflict."[28]

As Catherine Lotrionte points out in her article for this volume, there are three bodies of international law governing cyberspace: the norm of nonintervention, the laws governing the use of force (*jus ad bellum*), and the laws governing the conduct of armed conflict (*jus in bello*).[29] Article 2(4) of the UN Charter prohibits threat or use of force against states while Article 51 allows for individual or collective self-defense if an armed attack occurs. The legality of Stuxnet thus revolves around definitions of self-defense, use of force, and armed attacks. These definitions are contested for traditional kinetic conflicts, and their application to cyberspace is likewise subject to political and legal wrangling.

There are at least three approaches to the question of armed attack in cyber operations. The first looks at the type of weapon used and asks whether it produced the physical effects associated with military coercion. The second takes a target-based approach and would classify any attack on critical infrastructure—no matter the out-come—as an armed attack given the potential for damage. The third is a consequences-based model that looks at the severity, immediacy, and directness of harm of the digital assault on the victim.

The norm of nonintervention is concerned with coercion and interference. If the action is designed to prevent a state from do-ing something it is legally free to do, then it is coercive. But if it is a reaction against something illegal, then it could be considered a lawful countermeasure. Lawful countermeasures must meet certain requirements: countermeasures must induce the offending state to comply with international law; the state conducting the countermea-sure must show that either it has been injured or is acting on behalf of the international community; the state must call upon the offending state to comply with international law before using countermeasures; the use of countermeasures would need to stop once the offend-ing state complies with its obligations; and countermeasures must be proportionate.

While Lotrionte argues that under these conditions, and assum-ing Iran was in violation of the Non-Proliferation Treaty and various UN resolutions, Stuxnet could be considered a lawful countermea-sure, she also notes that there is a dispute over whether a counter-measure can violate the prohibition of the use of force against states. Mary Ellen O'Connell and Reyam El Molla, for example, argue that "international law does not permit the use of military force without United Nations Security Council authorization for arms control of any kind."[30] Sanctions and other actions against Iran's nuclear pro-gram would be considered legal countermeasures, but in O'Connell and El Molla's framing, Stuxnet—which would be considered a use of force against Iran—could only be used in response to an armed attack.

The other legal justification for Stuxnet would be in collective or individual self-defense outside of war. Lotrionte argues that Iran's nuclear program might represent a "threat to use force," in which case the United States deploying a forcible countermeasure such as Stux-net might be warranted if it could demonstrate necessity, meaning that only a forcible countermeasure is available to stop Iran's illegal nuclear program. Any countermeasure would have to stop once the threat ceased. In addition to necessity, a forcible countermeasure would have to be proportionate in terms of size, target, and duration. Attacks also cannot damage innocent third parties.

The design of Stuxnet appears to have in part been shaped by these legal concerns. In reference to Stuxnet, Richard Clarke commented, "It just says lawyers all over it."[31] The virus, for example, limited its own ability to spread. Each infected device would only spread Stuxnet to three other systems. Moreover, Stuxnet only affected Siemens SCADA programmable logic controller (PLC) software that matched a complex set of parameters. And as noted before, the code contained a "kill switch" mechanism. On June 24, 2012, all copies of the virus ceased to function.

HOW STUXNET MAY CHANGE THE LEGAL LANDSCAPE

International law, Lotrionte notes, develops deliberately and conservatively. Individual state actions or "inconsistent behaviors" do not help form customary international law. For a new rule to develop, there must be state behavior and *opinio juris*. As a result, Stuxnet by itself does not help create new law. Rather, to begin to shape the development of international law, the United States and Israel would have to publicly acknowledge the attack and provide their own justifications for its legality or why it use falls under an exception to the rules against the use of force.

As Ashley Deeks points out, the large majority of state practice in cyberspace is done secretly: "Far more than many other areas of geopolitical activity, states' actual conduct in the cyber arena remains unknown and, to a large extent, unknowable to other states."[32] Under these conditions, customary law will be slow to develop, and so Stuxnet's impact on international law may be most directly felt through the numerous diplomatic efforts to determine definitions for the use of force, aggression, intervention, and self-defense. These efforts include US declaratory policy with regard to cyberattacks and self-defense; the drafting of and state reactions to the *Tallinn Manual on*

International Law Applicable to Cyber Warfare, an academic, nonbinding study on how international law applies to cyber conflict and cyber-war; and discussions on norms and appropriate responses to cyber threats at the Association of Southeast Asian Nations (ASEAN), the Organization for Security and Co-operation in Europe (OSCE), and other multilateral fora. But, given the rapid pace of technological change, the competing interests of the major powers, the low visibility of attacks, disputes about events and outcomes, and difficulties in establishing attribution, this will be an uneven process.

International law and strategy are constantly interacting. As Matthew Waxman argues, "strategy generates reappraisal and revision of law, while law itself shapes strategy."[33] The drawing of legal lines has a distributive effect on power relations, and legal rules on cyberattacks have disparate strategic effects. The United States has interpreted Articles 2(4) and 51 in ways that prohibit certain types of destructive attacks but are more permissive for cyber espionage, coercion, and sabotage. But new technologies or adversary capabilities may change this strategic logic. In the future, a Stuxnet-like attack may no longer make strategic or legal sense. As a result, Washington might broaden or narrow legal definitions of use of force or armed attacks.

Foreign Reactions to Stuxnet

THERE HAS BEEN AN EXPLOSION of cybersecurity activity at the national and international level since Stuxnet came out into the open. At the national level, countries have been turning their attention to the development of doctrine, policies, and institutions necessary for cyber offensive operations. They have also continued the process of deterring, defending, and recovering from attacks. At the international level, discussions about norms and rules of the road are occurring at numerous multilateral, regional, and bilateral venues.

In the days, weeks, and months after the attack went public, Stuxnet woke up governments and businesses to the vulnerability of industrial systems. India, for example, was particularly hard-hit by Stuxnet infections, and the National Technical Research Organization (NTRO), India's technical intelligence agency, reportedly began drafting a report on how to mitigate the threat only days after the malware was discovered. The NTRO was later designated the lead agency in defending critical infrastructure, and, along with the Defense Intelligence Agency, was given the authority to conduct offensive operations. In 2015, after an almost three-year delay, Delhi announced the establishment of a national cyber coordinator in the prime minister's office.

It is difficult, however, to tease out how much recent activity is motivated by Stuxnet and how much is a reaction to the unrelenting pace of all types of cyberattacks in general and the Edward Snowden revelations, which began in 2013, in particular. In the United Kingdom, the British government had designated cybersecurity as a top-tier security threat in 2010, and armed forces minister Nick Harvey called for the need to develop offensive capabilities as a deterrent to destructive attacks.[34] The speech happened a few months after Stuxnet became public, but the idea that defense alone is unsustainable and that states must have the ability to attack predates the digital assault on Natanz.

For those on the receiving end of NSA cyber espionage intrusions, many of whom may one day be the targets of US offensive operations, the pressures to address cybersecurity challenges are even more intense. After the revelations, there was concern that the malware would negatively impact the United States' ability to convince other states of the need for norms of peaceful conduct in cyberspace if the other states believe Washington has already used cyberweapons. The United States would appear hypocritical and untrustworthy. But it is also true that many potential adversaries had been thinking about and developing offensive capabilities long before Stuxnet.[35]

REACTIONS FROM ALLIES, NGOs, AND OTHER NONSTATE ACTORS

The public reaction from friends and allies has been relatively muted, though it is likely that many have asked for clarification on Olympic Games behind closed doors. Israel has not taken credit for the operation, embracing a "cyber ambiguity" policy of neither denying nor admitting its use of cyber capabilities that mirrors its position on its nuclear weapons program. Yet several serving and former government officials have suggested the participation of the Israeli government. A video shown at a party celebrating the end of Lieutenant General Gabi Ashkenazi's tenure as IDF chief of staff, for example, listed his operational successes and included a reference to Stuxnet.[36] On a radio program discussing the malware Flame, Vice Premier and Minister of Strategic Affairs Moshe Ya'alon commented that Israel was blessed with superior technology: "These achievements of ours open all kinds of possibilities for us."[37]

Stuxnet appears to have added a degree of urgency to the development of doctrine, domestic innovation, and diplomatic platforms.

Policies that were in the works were completed on shorter timetables. The UK released its new Cyber Security Strategy in November 2011, and announced the formation of a Defense Cyber Operations Group, hosted by Government Communications Headquarters and involving Ministry of Defence forces, "to develop new tactics, techniques and plans to deliver military effects, including enhanced security, through operations in cyberspace."[38] The same month, the Foreign Ministry hosted the London Conference on Cyberspace, which started a process that has included conferences in Seoul, Budapest, and The Hague. Although the reference was eventually removed from the final agenda, reports suggest that the British Foreign Ministry intended the London Conference to frame "norms of behavior" for cyberspace.

In 2011, Germany introduced a new cybersecurity strategy and the Cyber-Abwehrzentrum, a defense facility in Bonn dedicated to defending the country's critical infrastructure, including its electricity and water supply. That same year, the German Foreign Ministry identified confidence-building measures (CBMs) as useful tools for promoting rules of conduct in cyberspace. Among the measures suggested were cybersecurity conferences and military CBMs such as exchanging information on doctrine, joint training, crisis hotlines, and law enforcement cooperation. In a background paper prepared for a 2011 G8 meeting in France, Germany suggested G8 leaders begin a discussion on behavioral norms for state-to-state activities that could possibly include the obligation to protect critical infrastructure.

While not coordinated or planned, looking across the activities of NGOs, academics, and other private actors, it is possible to discern a move to promoting distributed, decentralized, or multistakeholder security models. These models stem from both suspicion of the state and its "securitization" of cyberspace and an insistence that the dominant actors in cyberspace remain private actors, despite the sophistication of Stuxnet. Ron Deibert, director of the Citizen Lab at the University of Toronto, describes Stuxnet as part of the transformation of cyberspace into a national security domain and offers a model of security based on "decentralized and mixed authority and a multitude of overlapping responsibilities."[39] A report by the Atlantic Council and the Swedish National Defense College applies a "multistakeholder-centric approach" to confidence-building measures, an area usually the sole purview of states. Companies, NGOs, civil society, and others can play a role in strengthening transparency and confidence.[40] Jason Healey of Columbia University and the Atlantic Council argues that a successful cyber strategy must "accept the central role of the nonstate actors and the private sector and then work outwards from that core of strength."[41]

In an example of the process described and promoted by Deibert and the Atlantic Council, Microsoft has proposed six norms to reduce "to reduce the possibility that ICT [information and communications technology] products and services could be used, abused, or exploited by nation states as part of offensive operations." These norms include a prohibition on states targeting companies to insert vulnerabilities; a policy of reporting vulnerabilities to companies and not stockpiling; developing weapons that are precise, limited, and not reusable; and an avoidance of cyber operations that create mass effects.[42] Yet, because Stuxnet relied on an exploit tied to Microsoft's update process, the software giant also has an economic interest in reversing the perception that it cooperated with US military and intelligence agencies, either voluntarily or under legal authority.

REACTIONS FROM ADVERSARIES

CHINA

The attacks exposed China's sense of vulnerability to cyberattacks on industrial control systems (ICS). Many Chinese installations were infected by Stuxnet, and in the months after its discovery, the Chinese press ran several stories on China's dependence on foreign-supplied PLCs and other industrial control systems. In December 2014, China established its first laboratory to work on information security for industrial control systems. According to the announcement of the lab's opening, Chinese systems are vulnerable to attack for at least three reasons: operators have low security awareness and industrial control systems are connected to the Internet; Chinese industry is heavily reliant on foreign suppliers for ICS and these suppliers have access to industry systems in order to service or update software; and the country lacks a testing range or simulation environment to prepare for and defend against attacks.

China has used the operation against Natanz as evidence that it was the United States that "militarized" cyberspace first. This trope is frequently deployed to undermine US legitimacy in efforts to promote the free flow of information, norms against industrial cyber espionage, and the multistakeholder approach to Internet governance. As J. Stapleton Roy notes in this volume, Stuxnet also reinforces Beijing's view that the United States is hypocritical in painting China as the largest threat to cybersecurity.[43]

Attempting to capitalize on a perceived international shift away from a US-centric international governance model, China, along with Russia, Tajikistan, and Uzbekistan, circulated an International Code of Conduct on Information Security for the consideration of UN member states in 2011. The Code of Conduct, which came two months before the London Conference, also sought to identify the rights and responsibilities of states in cyberspace, but in contrast to the normative or "soft law" approach of the United States and its allies, it was grounded in a more formal agreement. The Code called on states "Not to use information and communications technologies, including networks, to carry out hostile activities or acts of aggression, pose threats to international peace and security or proliferate information weapons or related technologies."[44]

Shortly after the first Snowden revelations, Beijing and Washington agreed to a bilateral cyber working group on June 20, 2013. In addition to addressing cyber espionage, the United States hoped the group would begin to discuss issues Stuxnet raised like the legitimacy of targeting critical infrastructure and thresholds for destructive attacks. The talks were suspended in May 2014, however, after the United States indicted five PLA officers for the cyber-enabled theft of intellectual property and business secrets.

RUSSIA

In Russia, Stuxnet was followed by a flurry of activity on both the domestic and international fronts. As Timothy Thomas notes in his chapter, after quickly rewriting the code that was running its ICS systems, Russia turned to domestic conventions and protocols to clarify concepts, doctrines, and responsibilities. These conventions included: Conceptual Views on the Activities of the Armed Forces of the Russian Federation in Information Space (2011); a presidential decree identifying, preventing, and eliminating the consequences of cyberattacks (January 2013); and a new cyberspace strategy (2013).[45] In early 2012, Russia's Deputy Prime Minister Dmitry Rogozin announced plans to create a new service in the Russian military. "We are discussing the creation of a cyber command," the defense minister said. "Russia is following the US and NATO, which established Cyber Commands long ago." This new organization remained a work in progress in April 2015.

At the international level, as noted above, Russia has worked closely with China on promoting the Code of Conduct for Information Security. There was some space between Beijing's and Moscow's positions, however, on the question of whether international humanitarian law was applicable to cyberspace. China reluctantly signed off on a 2013 report of the Group of Governmental Experts on Developments in the Field of Information and Telecommunications in the Context of International Security, asserting that international law and the UN Charter applied in cyberspace in part because Beijing was isolated from the fourteen other participants, including Russia.

There was also progress in bilateral discussions with the United States before talks were suspended due to the Ukraine crisis. In June 2011, the two sides agreed to share military views on cyberspace operations and to regularize information exchange between the Computer Emergency Response/Readiness Teams. They also agreed to use the existing crisis-prevention "hot line" to communicate about cybersecurity crises.[46]

IRAN

As the victim of the attack, Iran may be easiest case in which to draw a relatively straight line from Stuxnet to actions and behaviors. Hossein Mousavian, a former Iranian diplomat, told an audience at Fordham Law School, "The US, or Israel, or the Europeans, or all of them together, started war against Iran." "Iran decided to have…to establish a cyber-army," he continued, "and today, after four or five years, Iran has one of the most powerful cyber armies in the world."[47]

It is hard to confirm the numbers for investments and the size of cyber forces, but defensive and offensive capabilities are clearly an Iranian government priority. Prior to 2009, most cyber efforts were directed inward, focused on controlling information flows and exploiting platforms used by dissidents. In late 2011, some sources claimed Iran invested at least one billion dollars in cyber technology, infrastructure, and expertise. A more recent report claims that when President Hassan Rouhani took office in 2013, the funding allocation for cybersecurity was 42,073 million IRR. It jumped to 178,800 million IRR in 2014 and currently stands at 550,000 million IRR, an increase of more than 1200 percent in just three years.[48]

There is a similar upward trend in cyber forces. In November 2010, the Basij, the volunteer paramilitary, asserted that it had trained 1500 cyber warriors. In March 2012, the Iranian Revolutionary Guard Corps (IRGC) claimed it had recruited around 120,000 personnel over the last three years to combat "a soft cyber war against Iran." In early 2013, an IRGC general publically claimed Iran was the "fourth biggest cyber power among the world's cyber armies." And in early March 2012, Supreme Leader of Iran Ayatollah Ali Khameni publicly announced to state media the creation by decree of a new Supreme Council of Cyberspace charged "to oversee the defense of the Islamic Republic's computer networks and develop new ways of infiltrating or attacking the computer networks of its enemies."[49]

Cyberattacks launched from Iran throughout 2012 should also be considered a response to Stuxnet, an effort to signal to the US government that Tehran had developed its own capacities and that future attacks would have a cost. In August 2012, the Shamoon malware struck Saudi Aramco, Riyadh's state oil giant. Employee email was shut down and the company had to replace thirty thousand computers in order to rid its networks of the malware. Saudi Aramco supplies about a tenth of the world's oil, but the malware only damaged office computers and did not affect systems involved with technical operations. The company managed to put its networks back online almost two weeks after the attack. A subsequent attack damaged Rasgas, a joint venture between Qatar Petroleum and ExxonMobil and the second-biggest producer of liquefied natural gas in the world. Again, data was destroyed but production continued. A group calling itself the Cutting Sword of Justice claimed responsibility, but US officials believed Iran was behind the attacks.[50]

Between September 2012 and June 2013, an activist group called Izz ad-Din al-Qassam Cyber Fighters launched roughly two hundred Distributed Denial of Service (DDoS) attacks on almost fifty financial institutions, including SunTrust, JPMorgan Chase, CitiGroup, Wells Fargo, U.S. Bancorp, Capital One, PNC, and HSBC. Over time, the attacks grew more complex; the amount of data flooding websites grew massively, and it cost one bank close to ten million to get back online. Izz ad-Din al-Qassam claimed it was acting independently and in retaliation for "Innocence of Muslims," an anti-Islam video made by a California resident and uploaded to YouTube, but behind the scenes, US government officials and outside experts blamed Iran.[51]

Iran's capabilities improved as a result of government investment and attention as well as competition with and attack from the United States and Israel. In 2013, General Keith Alexander, the Director of the National Security Agency and the commander of US Cyber Command, left Fort Meade for a meeting with his counterpart in the United Kingdom's Government Communications Headquarters. Talking points, prepared for the meeting with Sir Iain Robert Lobban and leaked by Snowden, claimed Iran had "demonstrated a clear ability to learn from the capabilities and actions of others."[52]

In the months after Stuxnet, US friends, allies, and adversaries ramped up their cyber activities at home and as part of their international agendas. Some of the earliest work was specifically focused on the threats of a Stuxnet-like attack on industrial control systems—rewriting code, developing action plans for critical infrastructure, and appointing cyber coordinators. While Stuxnet remained a motivating factor, a host of other cybersecurity threats gave focus to policymaking efforts in the following years.

Stuxnet and the US Global Cyber Agenda

Published by the Obama administration after Stuxnet became public, the 2011 International Strategy for Cyberspace brought previously stated goals and priorities together in one document. The agenda for cyberspace described by the White House includes: protecting freedom of expression, promoting innovation and protecting intellectual property, supporting the multistakeholder model, preventing attacks and crime, and enabling military operations. The strategy identifies the use of diplomacy, defense, and development "to promote an open, interoperable, secure, and reliable information and communications infrastructure."[53]

At the same time, Stuxnet undermined the trust and confidence of Internet users globally in the United States as a steward of the values of openness, globalism, security, and resilience. Yet Stuxnet's impact on Internet freedom and governance debates was, as Merritt Baer and Tim Maurer argue, indirect.[54] If the attack on Natanz lit the spark of wariness, the Snowden revelations acted as a barrel of gasoline dropped on the fire of distrust. Or, as the Internet governance scholar Milton Mueller puts it, "Stuxnet/Flame got people thinking. NSA/Snowden sealed the deal."[55]

STUXNET AND THE INTERNATIONAL CYBER GOVERNANCE DEBATE

Washington and its allies favor the "multistakeholder" model of Internet governance: a bottom-up policy process that includes organizations representing a diverse array of technical experts, governments, businesses, civil society, and individual users. Authoritarian states like China, Russia, and Iran are pushing for a state-centric approach, with greater involvement of multilateral organizations like the UN's International Telecommunication Union (ITU). In addition, many developing countries, which often lack independent civil society actors or businesses capable of participating in multistakeholder governance, prefer multilateral organizations where governments are the primary actors.

The ITU did seize on Stuxnet, and cybersecurity more generally, as justification for playing a greater role in Internet governance. "[Stuxnet] should serve as a wake-up call for all nations regarding the threat we all face," said Hamadoun Touré, the former secretary general of the ITU, adding that an arms control treaty was his priority.[56] The ITU also played an indirect role in exposing Flame. The ITU asked Kaspersky to investigate the malware that was wiping data on computers in Iran and, in the course of that investigation, the company uncovered Flame. In May 2012, the ITU publicized Flame in a warning to member states, calling for "global collaboration to tackle cybersecurity threats."[57] The request for the investigation and the global warning were both unprecedented, and James Lewis has argued that this was not a coincidence, but rather "consistent with an effort at political manipulation to win support at upcoming multilateral meetings on Internet governance."[58]

Cybersecurity was indeed a contentious issue at the 2012 World Conference on International Telecommunications and the 2014 International Telecommunication Union Plenipotentiary Conference, but neither of those conferences produced any real change in how the Internet is governed. The US strategy remains to try to limit the ITU's role to education and capacity-building. As Baer and Maurer note, the most lasting effect may be that Stuxnet forced what had been two fairly distinct communities—cybersecurity and Internet governance experts—into closer contact. Previously, both had been peripheral to each other. Now, the two policy discourses are intertwined.

Long-Term Consequences of Stuxnet

EVALUATING THE LONG-TERM CONSEQUENCES OF Stuxnet depends in part on how revolutionary the attack appears. Certainly, many of those who worked on decoding the malware described the attack code as a radical change. "I'd call it groundbreaking," said Roel Schouwenberg of Kaspersky Lab.[59] This sense of transformation stemmed in large part from the fact that Stuxnet was designed to do physical damage to an industrial control system. As Patrick Fitzgerald, a researcher with Symantec, put it, "Giving an attacker control of industrial systems like a dam, a sewage plant or a power station is extremely unusual and makes this a serious threat with huge real world implications. It has changed everything."[60] In a 2014 Pew Survey of more than 1600 Internet experts, 61 percent said that a major attack, one that caused widespread harm to a nation's security and capacity to defend itself and its people, was likely to happen by 2025 (this is not much different, however, from the responses to the 2004 survey, when 66 percent believed there would be at least one devastating attack on information infrastructure or a power grid within ten years).[61]

Despite media proclamations of the dawning of a new era, James Lewis is firm that Stuxnet was part of a larger, ongoing contest, not a dramatic break from the past. "Notions of blowback, collateral damage, or opening a Pandora's Box do not make sense in the context of how cyber-attack techniques have been used and have evolved over the last three decades," Lewis argues. "Stuxnet and Flame were not apocalyptic, not particularly new, and not the dawn of some new era of warfare."[62]

Dorothy Denning argues that while Stuxnet was clearly an advance over previous cyberattacks, to be a "game changer," it would have to make a "noticeable mark on the future." It could do so in Denning's estimation by inspiring the authors of Stuxnet to accelerate the development and deployment of cyberweapons targeting industrial control systems (ICS), and by motivating other countries to develop similar capabilities. Denning sees both of those outcomes as likely, and so considers Stuxnet a qualitative change.[63]

As with thinking about the impact on US foreign relations, it is difficult to pull out the consequences of Stuxnet and an attack on ICS specifically from the more general effects of all types of state-backed cyberattacks on the international system. While the balance may change over time, in the short- to medium-term, the effects of Stuxnet on international relations have been narrower than the impact on offensive cyber operations.

LONG-TERM CONSEQUENCES FOR THE INTERNATIONAL SYSTEM

The cyber revolution has stressed and reshaped many of the fundamental building blocks and processes of foreign relations. Cyberattacks blur the distinction between war and peacetime; erode the norm of sovereignty; advantage offense over defense; and create strategic ambiguity about intentions, capabilities, and actors. Moreover, the nuclear stalemate meant that great powers exercised some restraint in their dealings with each other. Cyberspace, in contrast, "has opened up a new sphere of activity enabling great powers to push the envelope."[64] They can now engage in a range of actions that fall below the threshold of an armed attack. Stuxnet is part of this larger trend but does not stand apart in its impact.

Stuxnet also has the potential to lower decisionmakers' inhibitions to the use of force. If policymakers see cyberattacks as low-risk, high-impact tools, like drones, they are more likely to feel comfortable in ordering their use. This is especially true if precise cyberattacks are viewed as more ethical weapons because they can degrade a target without creating physical damage or civilian fatalities.

Stuxnet also points to the rise of nonstate actors, and cybersecurity companies in particular, as important players in foreign policy. Bruce Schneier, the noted cryptologist and cybersecurity expert, wrote in October 2010, "My guess is that Stuxnet's authors, and its target, will forever remain a mystery."[65] Yet barely two years later, because of the work of dedicated teams of researchers at Symantec, Kaspersky, and Langner Group, the mission and workings of the malware had been almost completely unraveled. Private companies, including those involved in Stuxnet as well as Mandiant, FireEye, CrowdStrike, Cylance, and others, continue to play a large role in attribution. Cyber intelligence is, in the words of one official, "not solely a government game any longer."

Commercial actors force intelligence agencies to become more forthcoming about information on attacks presented to the public, and may help create international standards of attribution. It is no longer enough for governments to rely on a "just trust us" approach, releasing a little information but withholding details they fear will compromise technical means. Yet private firms also complicate signaling, as there tends to be an assumption that domestic companies are purely independent actors while companies headquartered in adversarial countries work collaboratively with their governments.

LONG-TERM CONSEQUENCES FOR OFFENSIVE CYBERWAR

Perhaps the most widespread but difficult to quantify impact of Stuxnet on offensive cyberattacks is the expansion of the "art of the possible." While many would have speculated that a successful attack on ICS was possible before Stuxnet, the digital assault on Natanz involved the creative and ambitious use of zero-days and new techniques in eye-opening and imagination-expanding ways. With creativity and enough resources, anything looks possible.

Proliferation—of techniques, malware, and ideas—remains a high concern. In 2014, reports from Symantec, CrowdStrike, and Kaspersky revealed a cyber espionage campaign named Energetic Bear or Dragonfly that had been in operation since 2011. Among the targets were energy grid operators, electricity generation firms, petroleum pipeline operators, and energy sector industrial control system equipment manufacturers. The attackers could have caused "damage or disruption to energy supplies."[66] The National Security Agency has warned that China, Russia, and several other countries already possess the ability to shut down a US power grid, and in November 2014, NSA Director and head of US Cyber Command Admiral Michael Rogers told Congress he expects US critical infrastructure to be attacked in the near- to medium-term. "It is only a matter of the when, not the if," Rogers said, "that we are going to see something traumatic."[67]

The sense of vulnerability that Stuxnet exposed—along with the Iranian cyberattacks on Saudi Aramco and Sands Casino and the North Korean cyberattacks on Sony Pictures that destroyed data—reinforced the perception of offense advantage in cyberspace, at least among US policymakers and operators. In March 2015, Admiral Rogers told the Senate Armed Services Committee that defense in cyberspace "will be both late to need and incredibly resource intensive." As a result, Rogers argued, "we also need to think about how can we increase our capacity on the offensive side, here, to get to that point of deterrence as you've raised."[68]

After seeing the effects of Stuxnet, many other countries around the world appear to have come to the same conclusion, raising the specter of an offense-dominant cyber environment marked by instability rather than deterrence stability. Cyber experts and policymakers had long expected the arrival of cyberweapons capable of destruction in the physical world. Now that such weapons are here, they must plan for and try to ameliorate the negative effects of a self-help world where offensive cyberweapons are the norm.

Notes

1. In December 2014, Bloomberg reported that Russian hackers were responsible for the Refahiye explosion on the Baku-Tbilisi-Ceyhan pipeline in 2008, two years before Stuxnet. Perhaps Stuxnet was not the Rubicon after all, but simply the first major incident of its type to receive public attention.

2.   David Albright, Paul Brannan, and Christina Walrond, "Did Stuxnet Take Out 1,000 Centrifuges at the Natanz Enrichment Plant? Preliminary Assessment," *ISIS Reports,* Institute for Science and International Security, December 22, 2010, http://isis-online.org/isis-reports/detail/did-stuxnet-take-out-1000-centrifuges-at-the-natanz-enrichment-plant/.

3.   David E. Sanger, "U.S. Rejected Aid for Israeli Raid on Iranian Nuclear Site," *New York Times,* January 10, 2009, http://www.nytimes.com/2009/01/11/washington/11iran.html.

4.   David E. Sanger, "Obama Order Sped Up Wave of Cyberattacks Against Iran," *New York Times,* June 12, 2012, http://www.nytimes.com/2012/06/01/world/middleeast/obama-ordered-wave-of-cyberattacks-against-iran.html.

5.   Rachel King, "Virus Aimed at Iran Infected Chevron Network," *Wall Street Journal,* November 9, 2012, http://www.wsj.com/articles/SB10001424127887324894104578107223667421796.

6.   Kim Zetter, *Count Down to Zero Day: Stuxnet and the Launch of the World's First Digital Weapon,* (New York: Crown Publishing, 2014).

7.   Robert McMillan, "How to Plan an Industrial Cyber-sabotage Operation: A Look at Stuxnet," *CSO,* September 20, 2010, http://www.csoonline.com/article/2136898/data-protection/how-to-plan-an-industrial-cyber-sabotage-operation--a-look-at-stuxnet.html.

8.   William J. Broad, John Markoff, and David E. Sanger, "Israeli Test on Worm Called Crucial in Iran Nuclear Delay," *New York Times,* January 15, 2011, http://www.nytimes.com/2011/01/16/world/middleeast/16stuxnet.html.

9.   See, for example, the controlled destruction of a generator in the Aurora Generator Test.

10.   Quoted in Ellen Nakashima, "Iran Blamed for Cyberattacks on U.S. Banks and Companies," *Washington Post,* September 21, 2012, http://www.washingtonpost.com/world/national-security/iran-blamed-for-cyberattacks/2012/09/21/afbe2be4-0412-11e2-9b24-ff730c7f6312_story.html.

11.   David Kushner, "The Real Story of Stuxnet," *IEEE Spectrum,* February 26, 2013, http://spectrum.ieee.org/telecom/security/the-real-story-of-stuxnet.

12.   Jason Ukman, "After Stuxnet, Waiting on Pandora's Box," *Washington Post,* September 20, 2011,http://www.washingtonpost.com/blogs/checkpoint-washington/post/after-stuxnet-waiting-on-pandoras-box/2011/09/20/gIQAOkw0hK_blog.html%20.

13.   Henry Kissinger and George P. Shultz, "The Iran Deal and Its Consequences," *Wall Street Journal,* April 7, 2015, http://www.wsj.com/articles/the-iran-deal-and-its-consequences-1428447582.

14.   Jonathan Steele, "Israel Asked US for a Green Light to Bomb Nuclear Sites in Iran," *Guardian* (London), January 11, 2009, http://guardian.co.uk/world/2008/sep/25/iran.israelandthepalestinians1.

15. David E. Sanger, James Glanz, and Jo Becker, "Around the World, Distress over Iran," *New York Times*, November 28, 2010, http://www.nytimes.com/2010/11/29/world/middleeast/29iran.html.

16. Mark Clayton, "Stuxnet: Ahmadinejad Admits Cyberweapon Hit Iran Nuclear Program," *Christian Science Monitor*, November 30, 2010, http://www.csmonitor.com/USA/2010/1130/Stuxnet-Ahmadinejad-admits-cyberweapon-hit-Iran-nuclear-program.

17. Albright, Brannan, and Walrond, "Did Stuxnet Take Out 1,000 Centrifuges?"; and David Albright, Paul Brannan, and Christina Walrond, "Stuxnet Malware and Natanz: Update of ISIS December 22, 2010 Report," February 15, 2011, http://isis-online.org/isis-reports/detail/stuxnet-malware-and-natanz-update-of-isis-december-22-2010-reportsupa-href1/.

18. Sanger, "Obama Order Sped Up Cyberattacks."

19. Ivanka Barzashka, "Are Cyber-Weapons Effective? Assessing Stuxnet's Impact on the Iranian Enrichment Programme," *RUSI Journal*, 158, no. 2(2013), http://www.tandfonline.com/doi/full/10.1080/03071847.2013.787735#abstract.

20. Glenn Greenwald and Ewen MacAskill, "Obama Orders US to Draw Up Overseas Target List for Cyber-attacks," *Guardian*, June 7, 2013, http://www.theguardian.com/world/2013/jun/07/obama-china-targets-cyber-overseas.

21. Ibid.

22. Merritt Baer, "National Security Law after Stuxnet," (paper presented at the Cyber Conflict Studies Association "Cyber Conflict After Stuxnet" Symposium, Washington, DC, November 2013).

23. Presidential Approval and Reporting of Covert Actions, National Security Act of 1947, 50 U.S.C. § 3093 (1947), https://www.law.cornell.edu/uscode/text/50/3093.

24. Jack Goldsmith, "What is the Domestic Legal Basis for Planned Cyberattacks in Syria?," *Lawfare Blog*, February 25, 2014, http://www.lawfareblog.com/2014/02/what-is-the-dor. mestic-legal-basis-for-planned-cyberattacks-in-syria/.

25. Iran signed the Non-Proliferation Treaty in 1968.

26. Eric Lorber, "Executive Warmaking Authority and Offensive Cyber Operations: Can Existing Legislation Successfully Constrain Presidential Power?," *University of Pennsylvania Journal of Constitutional Law* 15, no. 3 (2014): 961-1002, http://scholarship.law.upenn.edu/jcl/vol15/iss3/6.

27. Harold Hongju Koh, "International Law in Cyberspace," USCYBERCOM, Inter-Agency Legal Conference, Ft. Meade, MD, September 18, 2012, http://opiniojuris.org/2012/09/19/harold-koh-on-international-law-in-cyberspace/.

28. Greenwald and MacAskill, "Obama Orders Target List for Cyber-attacks."

29. Catherine Lotrionte, "Stuxnet: International Legal Considerations and Implications for International Law," *Cyber Conflict after Stuxnet: Essays from the Other Bank of the Rubicon*, (Washington, DC: Cyber Conflict Studies Association, 2016).

30. Mary Ellen O'Connell and Reyam El Molla, "The Prohibition of Use of Force Arms Control: The Case of Iran's Nuclear Program," *Penn State Journal of Law & International Affairs* 2, no. 2 (November 2013): 315-327.

31. Michael Joseph Gross, "A Declaration of Cyber-War," *Vanity Fair*, March 2011, http://www.vanityfair.com/news/2011/03/stuxnet-201104.

32. Ashley Deeks, "International Perspectives on Regulating Military Cyber Activity," *Net Politics Blog*, Council on Foreign Relations, June 3, 2015, http://blogs.cfr.org/cyber/2015/06/03/international-perspectives-on-regulating-military-cyber-activity/.

33. Matthew Waxman, "Cyber-Attacks and the Use of Force: Back to the Future of Article 2(4)," *Yale Journal of International Law* 36, no. 2 (2011): 421-459, http://www.yjil.org/print/volume-36-issue-2/cyber-attacks-and-the-use-of-force-back-to-the-future-of-article-24.

34. Peter Apps, "UK Needs Cyberattack Capability: Minister," Reuters, November 10, 2010, http://www.reuters.com/article/2010/11/10/us-britain-cyber-idUSTRE6A923Z20101110.

35. John Negroponte, Samuel Palmisano, and Adam Segal, "Defending an Open, Global, Secure, and Resilient Internet," Council on Foreign Relations Independent Task Force, June 2013, http://www.cfr.org/cybersecurity/defending-open-global-secure-resilient-internet/p30836.

36. Christopher Williams, "Israel Video Shows Stuxnet as One of its Successes," *Telegraph*, February 15, 2011, http://www.telegraph.co.uk/news/worldnews/middleeast/israel/8326387/Israel-video-shows-Stuxnet-as-one-of-its-successes.html.

37. Yaakov Katz, "IDF Admits to Using Cyber Space to Attack Enemies," *Jerusalem Post*, June 3, 2011, http://www.jpost.com/Defense/IDF-admits-to-using-cyber-space-to-attack-enemies.

38. "The UK Cyber Security Strategy: Protecting and Promoting the UK in a Digital World," November 2011, https://www.gov.uk/government/uploads/system/uploads/attachment_data/file/60961/uk-cyber-security-strategy-final.pdf.

39. Ron Deibert, "Distributed Security as Cyber Strategy: Outlining a Comprehensive Approach for Canada in Cyberspace," Canadian Defence & Foreign Affairs Institute, August 2012, https://citizenlab.org/wp-content/uploads/2012/08/CDFAI-Distributed-Security-as-Cyber-Strategy_-outlining-a-comprehensive-approach-for-Canada-in-Cyber.pdf.

40. Jason Healey, John C. Mallery, Klara Tothova Jordan, and Nathaniel V. Youd, "Confidence-Building Measures in Cyberspace: A Multistakeholder Approach for Stability and Security," Cyber Statecraft Initiative, Atlantic Council, November 5, 2014, http://www.atlanticcouncil.org/images/publications/Confidence-Building_Measures_in_Cyberspace.pdf.

41. Jason Healey, "A Nonstate Strategy for Saving Cyberspace," Atlantic Council Working Paper, May 2015, 5.

42. Angela McKay, Jan Neutze, Paul Nicholas, and Kevin Sullivan, "International Cybersecurity Norms: Reducing Conflict in an Internet-dependent World,"

Microsoft, December 2014, http://www.microsoft.com/en-us/download/details.aspx?id=45031.

43. J. Stapleton Roy, "Stuxnet and China," *Cyber Conflict after Stuxnet: Essays from the Other Bank of the Rubicon*, (Washington, DC: Cyber Conflict Studies Association, 2016).

44. UN General Assembly, "International Code of Conduct for Information Security," September 12, 2011, https://ccdcoe.org/sites/default/files/documents/UN-110912-CodeOfConduct_0.pdf.

45. Timothy Thomas, "Russia's Response to the Stuxnet Incident," *Cyber Conflict after Stuxnet: Essays from the Other Bank of the Rubicon*, (Washington, DC: Cyber Conflict Studies Association, 2016).

46. Howard Schmidt, "U.S. and Russia: Expanding the 'Reset' to Cyberspace," *White House Blog*, July 12, 2011, https://www.whitehouse.gov/blog/2011/07/12/us-and-russia-expanding-reset-cyberspace.

47. Quoted in Mark Clayton, "Cyber-war: In Deed and Desire, Iran Emerging as a Major Power," *Christian Science Monitor*, March 16, 2014, http://www.csmonitor.com/World/Passcode/2014/0316/Cyber-war-In-deed-and-desire-Iran-emerging-as-a-major-power.

48. "Iranian Internet Infrastructure and Policy Report," *Small Media*, February 2015, http://smallmedia.org.uk/sites/default/files/u8/IIIP_Feb15.pdf.

49. Natasha Bertrand, "Iran is Building a Non-nuclear Threat Faster than Experts 'Would Have Ever Imagined,'" *Business Insider*, March 27, 2015, http://www.businessinsider.com/irans-cyber-army-2015-3; Lt. Col. Eric K. Shafa, "Iran's Emergence as a Cyber Power," Strategic Studies Institute, August 20, 2014, http://www.strategicstudiesinstitute.army.mil/index.cfm/articles/Irans-emergence-as-cyber-power/2014/08/20.

50. "Text of Speech by Defense U.S. Secretary Leon Panetta," *DefenseNews*, October 12, 2012, http://www.defensenews.com/article/20121012/DEFREG02/310120001/Text-Speech-by-Defense-U-S-Secretary-Leon-Panetta; Jim Finkle, "Insiders Suspected in Saudi Cyber Attack," Reuters, September 7, 2012, http://in.reuters.com/article/2012/09/07/net-us-saudi-aramco-hack-idINBRE8860CR20120907.

51. Nicole Perloth and Quentin Hardy, "Bank Hacking Was the Work of Iranians, Officials Say," *New York Times*, January 8, 2013, http://www.nytimes.com/2013/01/09/technology/online-banking-attacks-were-work-of-iran-us-officials-say.html.; Nakashima, "Iran Blamed for Cyberattacks."

52. Kim Zetter, "The NSA Acknowledges What We All Feared: Iran Learns from US Cyberattacks," *Wired*, February 10, 2015, http://www.wired.com/2015/02/nsa-acknowledges-feared-iran-learns-us-cyberattacks/.

53. Executive Office of the President of the United States, "International Strategy for Cyberspace: Prosperity, Security, and Openness in a Networked World," (Washington, DC, May 2011), https://www.whitehouse.gov/sites/default/files/rss_viewer/international_strategy_for_cyberspace.pdf.

54. Merritt Baer and Tim Maurer, "Stuxnet and the Internet Governance Debate: The Growing Convergence of Internet Policy Issues and Communities," *Cyber Conflict after Stuxnet: Essays from the Other Bank of the Rubicon*, (Washington, DC: Cyber Conflict Studies Association, 2016).

55. Quoted in Ibid.

56. Joseph Menn, "Rules of Engagement for Cyberwars See Slow Progress," *Financial Times*, December 28, 2010, http://www.ft.com/cms/s/0/484ec672-12aa-11e0-b4c8-00144feabdc0.html.

57. Jim Finkle, "UN Agency Plans Major Warning on Flame Virus Risk," Reuters, May 12, 2012, http://www.reuters.com/article/2012/05/29/net-us-cyberwar-flame-idUSBRE84R0E420120529.

58. James Lewis, "In Defense of Stuxnet," *Military and Strategic Affairs*, 4, no. 3 (December 2012): 65-76.

59. Gregg Keizer, "Is Stuxnet the 'Best' Malware Ever?," *Computer World*, September 16, 2010, http://www.computerworld.com/article/2515757/malware-vulnerabilities/is-stuxnet-the--best--malware-ever-.html.

60. Paul Marks, "Why the Stuxnet Worm is Like Nothing Seen Before," *New Scientist*, January 18, 2011, http://www.newscientist.com/article/dn19504-why-the-stuxnet-worm-is-like-nothing-seen-before.html?DCMP=OTC-rss&nsref=science-in-society#.VV4Rxk9VhBc.

61. Lee Rainie, Janna Anderson, and Jennifer Connolly, "Cyberattacks Likely to Increase," *Pew Research Center*, October 29, 2014, http://www.pewinternet.org/2014/10/29/cyber-attacks-likely-to-increase/; Lee Rainie, Janna Anderson, and Susannah Fox, "The Future of the Internet I," *Pew Research Center*, January 9, 2005, http://www.pewinternet.org/2005/01/09/the-future-of-the-internet-i/.

62. Lewis, "In Defense of Stuxnet," 65, 75.

63. Dorothy E. Denning, "Stuxnet: What Has Changed?," *Future Internet* 4, no. 3 (2012): 672-687.

64. Tim Maurer, "The Future of War: Cyber is Expanding the Clausewitzian Spectrum of Conflict," *Foreign Policy*, November 13, 2014, http://foreignpolicy.com/2014/11/13/the-future-of-war-cyber-is-expanding-the-clausewitzian-spectrum-of-conflict/.

65. Bruce Schneier, "The Story Behind the Stuxnet Virus," *Forbes*, October 7, 2010, http://www.forbes.com/2010/10/06/iran-nuclear-computer-technology-security-stuxnet-worm.html.

66. "Emerging Threat: Dragonfly / Energetic Bear – APT Group," Symantec, June 30, 2014, http://www.symantec.com/connect/blogs/emerging-threat-dragonfly-energetic-bear-apt-group.

67. Jamie Crawford, "The U.S. Government Thinks China Could Take Down the Power Grid," CNN, November 21, 2014, http://www.cnn.com/2014/11/20/politics/nsa-china-power-grid/.

68. Hearing to receive testimony on US Strategic Command, US Transportation Command, and US Cyber Command, United States Senate, Armed Services Committee, March 19, 2015, http://www.armed-services.senate.gov/imo/media/doc/15-30%20-%203-19-15.pdf.

The Stuxnet Story

"What Was Stuxnet and What Are Its Hidden Lessons on the Ethics of Cyberweapons?" by P.W. Singer[1]

RALPH LANGNER IS A JOVIAL fellow with a quick wit whose sense of whimsy is perhaps best illustrated by the fact that he wears cowboy boots. Wearing cowboy boots should not be all that notable, until one realizes that Langner is not from Texas, but Germany, and is not a cowboy, but a computer specialist. Langner is also incredibly inquisitive. It was this combination that led him to play a role in the discovery of one of the most notable weapons in history—and not just cyber history, but history overall.

Since 1988, Langner and his team of security experts had been advising on the safety of large-scale installations. Their special focus was industrial control systems: computer systems like SCADA (short for "supervisory control and data acquisition") that monitor and run industrial processes. SCADA is used in everything from the management and operation of power plants to the manufacture of candy wrappers.

In 2010, like many other industrial control and cybersecurity experts around the world, Langner grew concerned about a cyber "worm" of unknown origin that was spreading across the world and embedding itself in these control systems. Thousands of computers in places like India and the United States had been infected. But the bulk of the infections (roughly 60 percent) were in Iran. This led many experts to infer that either Iran had particularly poor cyber defenses for its SCADA-related programs, which made them more vulnerable, or a virus had initially targeted some site in Iran and, as one report put it, "subsequently failed in its primary purpose and run amok, spreading uncontrollably to unintended targets all over the world, and thus demonstrating how indiscriminate and destructive cyber weapons were likely to be."[1]

Both turned out to be far from the case. Various teams of cyber experts from around the world began to dissect the code of "Stuxnet," as it became known, and debates grew over its origin and targets. Curious, the more Langner and his team explored it, the more interested they became. It was a wonderfully complex piece of malware like none the world had ever seen. It had at least four new "zero-days" (previously unknown vulnerabilities), utilized digital signatures with the private keys of two certificates stolen from separate well-known companies, and worked on all Windows operating systems down to the decade-old Windows 95 edition. The number of new zero-days particularly stood out. Hackers prize zero-days and do not like to reveal them when they do not have to. To use four at once was unprecedented and almost illogical, given that one new open door is enough. It was a pretty good sign that Stuxnet's makers had enormous resources and wanted to be absolutely certain they would penetrate their target.

Stuxnet also slipped by the Windows defenses using the equivalent of a stolen passport. To gain access to the "kernel," or operating system's control system, Stuxnet had to install a component that could talk to the kernel. The authors chose to target a device driver, a common tool that allows hardware devices to interact with the operating system. Windows uses a scheme of digital signatures to allow trusted hardware manufacturers to write device drivers that are trusted by the operating system. Unsigned drivers raise an alert for the user, while signed drivers do not. The drivers in Stuxnet were signed by two real companies in Taiwan, indicating that the authors had access to the secret signing keys—most likely stolen. Again, this is a rare style of attack: stolen signing keys are incredibly powerful, would have been well-protected, and would be very valuable in any illicit market.

Rather than being truly infectious, the malware's DNA revealed something even more interesting: Stuxnet was hunting for something in particular. As Langner delved deeper, he discovered that Stuxnet was not going after computers or even Windows software in general, but a specific type of program used in Siemens's WinCC/PCS 7 SCADA control software. Indeed, if this software was not present, the worm had built-in controls to become inert. In addition, rather than trying to spread as widely as possible, as was the goal with past worms, Stuxnet allowed each infected computer to spread the worm to no more than three others. It even came with a final safeguard: a self-destruct mechanism that caused it to basically erase itself in 2012. Whoever made Stuxnet not only had a specific target in mind, but did not want the code lingering in the wild forever.[2] This was a very different worm, indeed.

But what was the target? This was the true mystery. Here Langner's background working with industrial firms proved particularly useful. He figured out that Stuxnet was only going after a specific industrial controller, manufactured by Siemens, configured to run a series of nuclear centrifuges. But the target was not just any old nuclear centrifuge you might have lying around the house: only a "cascade" of centrifuges of a certain size and number (984) linked together. Not so coincidentally, this was the exact setup at the Natanz nuclear facility, a suspected site in Iran's illicit nuclear weapons program.

Things got especially tricky once Stuxnet found its way into this target (it was later revealed that the delivery mechanism was infiltration through Iranian nuclear scientists' own laptops and memory sticks). The attack did not shut down the centrifuges in any obvious manner. Instead, it ran a series of subroutines. One, known as a "man in the middle," caused tiny adjustments in pressure inside the centrifuges. Another manipulated the speed of the centrifuges' spinning rotors, causing them to alternately slow down and then speed back up, throwing the rotors out of whack and ruining their work. On top of this, every so often the malware would push the centrifuge speeds past the designed maximum. So the centrifuges were not just failing to produce refined uranium fuel; they were frequently breaking down and grinding to a halt from the damaging vibrations that the various random surges caused. At other times, the machines were literally spinning out of control and exploding.

The effect, Langner wrote, was "as good as using explosives" against the facility.[3] In fact, it was better. The victim had "no clue of being under a cyber attack."[4] For more than a year, Stuxnet had been inside Iranian networks, but the nuclear scientists initially thought their facility was just suffering from a series of random breakdowns. The scientists kept replacing the broken centrifuges with new ones, which would then become infected and break again.[5] Soon, though, they wondered whether they were being sold faulty parts or were suffering from some kind of hardware sabotage. But the machines checked out perfectly every time, except for the fact that nothing was working the way it should.

This was perhaps the most insidious part of Stuxnet: it was an integrity attack *par excellence*. Stuxnet didn't just corrupt the process; it hid its effects from the operators. It exploited not just technical vulnerabilities, but their all-too-human trust that the computer systems would accurately and honestly describe what was taking place. For a long period of time, the Iranian engineers did not even suspect a cyberattack—their systems were air-gapped from the web. Moreover, up to this point, worms and viruses had always had an obvious effect on the computer, not the hardware. Eventually, the attacks had another, human effect: the Iranian scientists suffered low morale, under the impression that they could not do anything right. Seventy years earlier, a bunch of Americans had built an atomic bomb using slide rulers, and they could not even get their modern-day centrifuges to work. Overall, Langner likened the Stuxnet effect to the cyber version of "Chinese water torture."[6]

When Langer revealed his findings on his blog, the little-known German researcher quickly became an international celebrity. First, he had exposed a top-secret campaign of sabotage (later revealed in the US media to have been the result of a collaborative effort between US and Israeli intelligence agencies, known as "Olympic Games"), and second, it was a find of global importance.[7] A new kind of weapon long speculated about but never seen—a specially-designed cyberweapon—had finally been used.

But when it came time to weigh the new weapon, the debate diverged. Judith Donath of Harvard University described Stuxnet as a demonstration of a new kind of weapon that could only get better: "The musket of cyberwarfare. What will be its rifle? Its AK-47? Its atomic bomb?"[8]

Others worried that these better weapons would promote a new kind of escalation and global risk. "Stuxnet was the absolute game changer," wrote cyber thinker Mikko Hypponen. "We are entering an arms race where countries start stocking weapons, only it isn't planes and nuclear reactors they're stocking, but it's cyberweapons."[9]

And still others were concerned of the opposite: not enough people took notice of this "opening shot in a war we will all lose," as Leslie Harris of the Center for Democracy and Technology calls it.[10] Stuxnet was all of these things, perhaps, but it was also notable for another reason: this nasty little worm was a superb illustration of how ethics can be applied to cyberwar.

There is the popular notion that "all is fair in love and war," but the reality is that there are actually a series of strict guidelines that are supposed to shape behavior in war—what 1600s legal thinker Hugo Grotius called *jus in bello* ("Laws in War"). The two biggest laws are proportionality and discrimination. The law of proportionality states that the suffering and devastation caused, especially collateral damage to unintended targets, cannot outweigh whatever harm prompted the conflict. If the other side stole your cow, you cannot justifiably nuke their city. The law of discrimination maintains that the sides must distinguish legitimate targets from those that should not be targeted (be they civilians or wounded) and do their utmost only to cause harm to the intended, legitimate targets.

Stuxnet stood out as a new kind of weapon designed to cause physical damage via cyber means. Its makers wanted it to break things in the real world through action only on digital networks. This was novel enough. But what really stands out compared to traditional weapons is how small its physical impact was, especially compared to the intense stakes. The target was a nuclear bomb-making program, one that had already been targeted by diplomatic efforts and economic sanctions. While it is certainly debatable whether preemptive action against the Iranian program is justifiable, this is when the question of proportionality becomes relevant. Stuxnet broke nothing other than the nuclear centrifuges, which had been illegally obtained by Iran to conduct illicit research. Moreover, it neither hurt nor killed anyone. In comparison, when Israel attempted to obstruct Iraqi nuclear research in 1981, its forces dropped sixteen 2,000-pound bombs on a research site during "Operation Opera," leveling it and killing eleven soldiers and civilians.

But discrimination also matters when judging the ethics of these attacks. At face value, Stuxnet would seem to have been incredibly indiscriminant. While limited in its promiscuity compared to prior malware, this was a worm that still got around. It infected not just targets in Iran but thousands of computers across the world that had nothing to do with Iran or nuclear research. Many lawyers see this facet of cyberweapons as proof of their inherent violation of "prevailing codes of international laws of conflict, as they go beyond just the original target and deliberately target civilian personnel and infrastructure."[11] Yet this may be an erroneous interpretation, outdated for the cyber age. While Stuxnet lacked discretion under the old way of thinking, its very design prevented harm to anyone and anything beyond the intended target. This kind of discrimination was something never previously possible in a weapon. As George Lucas, a philosopher at the US Naval Academy, wrote in an assessment of Stuxnet's ethics, "Unless you happen to be running a large array of exactly 984 Siemens centrifuges simultaneously, you have nothing to fear from this worm."[12]

In effect, judging the ethics of Stuxnet and cyberweapons more generally turns on which part of the story you care about most. Do you focus on the fact that this new kind of weapon permitted a preemptive attack and in so doing touched thousands of people and computers who had nothing to do with Iran or nuclear research? Or do you focus on the fact that the cyber strike caused far less damage than any previous comparable attack and that the weapon was so discriminating it essentially gave new meaning to the term? Are you a cyberweapon "half-full" or "half-empty" kind of person?

History may render the ultimate judgment of Stuxnet, however. As Ralph Langner put it, the fascinating new weapon he discovered "could be considered a textbook example of a 'just war' approach. It didn't kill anyone. That's a good thing. But I am afraid this is only a short-term view. In the long run it has opened Pandora's box."[13]

Notes

1. George R. Lucas, Jr., "Permissible Preventive Cyberwar: Restricting Cyber Conflict to Justified Military Targets," in *The Ethics of Information Warfare*, eds. Luciano Floridi and Mariarosaria Taddeo, (Springer International Publishing; New York, 2014), 79. A study of the spread of Stuxnet was undertaken by a number of international computer security firms, including Symantec Corporation. Their report, "W32.Stuxnet Dossier," compiled by noted computer security experts Nicolas Falliere, Liam O'Murchu, and Eric Chien, and released in February 2011, showed that the main countries affected during the early days of the infection were Iran, Indonesia, and India: http://www.symantec.com/content/en/us/enterprise/media/security_response/whitepapers/w32_stuxnet_dossier.pdf.

2. Lucas, "Permissible Preventive Cyberwar."

3. Ralph Langner, "Better than Bunker Busters: The Virtual Chinese Water Torture," *Langner.com*, November 15, 2010, http://www.langner.com/en/2010/11/15/better-than-bunker-busters-the-virtual-chinese-water-torture/.

4. Ibid.

5. Ralph Langer, quoted in Mark Clayton, "How Stuxnet Cyber Weapon Targeted Iran Nuclear Plant," *Christian Science Monitor*, November 16, 2010, http://www.csmonitor.com/USA/2010/1116/How-Stuxnet-cyber-weapon-targeted-Iran-nuclear-plant.

6. Ibid.

7. David E. Sanger, "Obama Order Sped Up Wave of Cyberattacks against Iran," *New York Times*, June 1, 2012, http://www.nytimes.com/2012/06/01/world/middleeast/obama-ordered-wave-of-cyberattacks-against-iran.html.

8   Suzanne Merkleson, "The FP Survey: The Internet," *Foreign Policy* (September–October 2011), 116.

9. Mikko Hypponen, quoted in Isabelle de Pommereau, "How Estonians Became Pioneering Cyberdefenders" *Christian Science Monitor*, June 8, 2011, http://www.csmonitor.com/World/Europe/2011/0608/How-Estonians-became-pioneering-cyberdefenders.

10. Leslie Harris, quoted in "The FP Survey," 116.

11. Neil C. Rowe, "Ethics of Cyber War Attacks," in *Cyber Warfare and Cyber Terrorism*, edited by Lech J. Janczewski and Andrew M. Colarik (Hershey, PA: Information Science Reference, 2008), 109.

12. George R. Lucas, Jr., "Permissible Preventive Cyberwar: Restricting Cyber Conflict to Justified Military Targets," opening address for a UNESCO-sponsored conference on Cyber War and Ethics at the University of Hertfordshire, Hatfield, England, July 1, 2011, www.elac.ox.ac.uk/downloads/Permissible Preventive Cyberwar UNESCO 2011.pdf.

13. Ralph Langner quoted in Mark Clayton, "From the Man Who Discovered Stuxnet, Dire Warnings One Year Later," *Christian Science Monitor*, September 22, 2011, http://www.csmonitor.com/USA/2011/0922/From-the-man-who-discovered-Stuxnet-dire-warnings-one-year-later.

Stuxnet and Legal/ Governance Frameworks

"Stuxnet: International Legal Considerations and Implications for International Law" by Catherine Lotrionte

SINCE THE LAUNCH OF STUXNET, there seems to have been an endless debate about the scope of a state's right to use force in cyberspace, including in a preemptive manner against imminent attacks by a state. The debate predates the events of Stuxnet, but Stuxnet sharpened its focus and gave it greater operational urgency. While cyber operations have been conducted in the past, most of those past efforts have focused mainly at disrupting Internet access (e.g., the 2008 Russia-Georgia conflict) or stealing government or corporate secrets (e.g., allegations that China has conducted economic and political espionage against the United States). Stuxnet was unprecedented in that it was conducted by a state against a sector of another state's critical infrastructure. It was the first time a cyber tool was used without an accompanying conventional strike to cause physical damage.

While an important strand of the debate has taken place in academic journals and public forums, another strand has developed largely away from the public gaze, within and between governments, about what the appropriate principles are, and ought to be, in respect to such conduct. Insofar as these discussions have informed the practice of states and their appreciations of legality, they carry particular weight, being material both to the crystallization and development of customary international law and to the interpretation of treaties. Unfortunately, no state has acknowledged its part in the cyber operation against Iran or provided a legal justification for those actions. Therefore, any legal analysis of Stuxnet must rely on certain assumptions. While Iran was initially silent about Stuxnet, the Iranian foreign affairs minister criticized the cyberattacks against Iran's nuclear facility in a September 2012 address to the UN Security Council (UNSC). He described the incident as a "manifestation of nuclear terrorism and consequently a grave violation of the principles of [the] UN Charter and international law."[1]

This article will provide a legal analysis of the Stuxnet operation under international law based upon current interpretations of cyberattacks and cyberwarfare under international law. This article does this based on the following assumptions: (1) one or more states carried out the Stuxnet operation against Iran; (2) the goal of Stuxnet was at least partially achieved in that it caused damage to the Iranian nuclear facility at Natanz, setting back the state's nuclear enrichment program by at least months, if not years; and (3) international law applies in the cyber domain. The article also discusses the implications for states' conduct of cyberattacks in the future and what challenges have to be overcome in order to establish an adequate regime of international law to govern cyber conflict.

Aspects of these otherwise largely intra- and intergovernmental discussions on the legal aspects of uses of force have periodically become publicly visible through official statements and speeches, evidence provided to governmental committees, reports of such committees, and similar documents. Other aspects have to be deduced from the practices of states—which, given the sensitivities, are sometimes opaque. In recent years the public remarks of senior Obama administration legal officials have illuminated elements of the debate in a US context related to the use of force in cyberspace in general and the principle of self-defense specifically, including comments by Harold Koh, the Department of State legal advisor. Based on previous

US state practice in the area of use of force and recent public statements and published strategies by US administrations, this article will discuss the international legal considerations related to Stuxnet and the implications for international law.

We must first be clear about the sources of international law. Law formulates the values of the community. International law reflects not the values of one nation, but the consensus of values that all nations profess. To discover the rules of international law, we must seek the values that states generally accept, and give weight to their practices only insofar as they provide evidence of that acceptance.

The statute of the International Court of Justice (ICJ) declares that the court, to decide cases in accordance with international law, shall apply:

(a) International conventions, whether general or particular, establishing rules expressly recognized by the contesting states;

(b) international custom, as evidence of a general practice accepted as law;

(c) the general principles of law recognized by civilized nations; and

(d) . . . judicial decisions and the teachings of the most highly qualified publicists of the various nations, as subsidiary means for the determination of rules of law.[2]

The use of the words "recognized" and "accepted" in this formulation emphasizes the importance of the subjective factor in appraising the value of material evidence of the law in conventions, practices, principles, precedents, and commentaries.

INTERNATIONAL LAW'S APPLICABILITY
TO CYBER OPERATIONS

The scope and manner of international law's applicability to state behavior on the Internet has remained unsettled since the advent of the technology, posing a fundamental challenge for states grappling with related issues. Indeed, when current international legal norms emerged, the Internet was not in the thoughts of those drafting relevant treaties or the states engaging in the applicable practice that constituted customary law. Certainly, state practice has outpaced the terms of the treaties and customary norms that have formed the basis of the governing legal regime.

The first question is thus whether existing international law applies to the Internet and, if so, which laws, how, and under the auspices of which international legal organization. Certainly, states have been concerned about this legal ambiguity, especially given the reports of the Stuxnet operation against the Iranian nuclear facility in Natanz, the cyberattacks against the oil company Saudi Aramco, allegations of Chinese cyber economic espionage against US companies, and the NSA's PRISM program. In 2011, in recognition of the lack of clarity related to the controlling laws, the United States published its International Strategy for Cyberspace, setting forth its position on the matter, stating, "Long-standing international norms guiding State behavior – in time of peace and conflict – also apply to cyberspace."[3] In a speech at Cyber Command, then–legal advisor to the State Department Harold Koh reiterated the US position that international law in general and the UN Charter principle and the laws of war in particular are applicable in cyberspace.

Most recently, UN members of the Group of Governmental Experts on Developments in the Field of International and Telecommunications in the Context of International Security (UNGGE), representing fifteen states, including Russia, the United States, and China, agreed that the UN Charter principles and, more generally, international law, apply in cyberspace. The International Court of Justice, in articulating customary international law, held that both Articles 2(4) and 51 of the UN Charter regarding the prohibition on the use of force and self-defense respectively apply to "any use of force, regardless of the weapons employed."[4] In sum, the fact that computers and software are used in an operation has no bearing on whether the operation was a "use of force" or whether a state can use force in self-defense.

For matters related to espionage and conflict in cyberspace, there is well-established international law governing the domain. This body of international law generally encompasses (1) the norm of nonintervention; (2) *jus ad bellum*, the international law governing the resort to force by states; (3) and *jus in bello*, the international law regulating the conduct of armed conflict (the laws of war or international humanitarian law). These laws are codified in treaty and customary international law established over years of state practice. For the purposes of Stuxnet, because the United States is not in a state of "armed conflict" with Iran, those laws related to *jus in bello* are not relevant. They will be mentioned in this article only to give the reader a sense of what the international rules would be if the controversy between the United States and Iran did escalate into "armed conflict." These rules would apply to cyber operations during an armed conflict just as they apply to conventional armed conflicts. Furthermore, while Stuxnet is distinguishable from an espionage operation, it is useful to begin by analyzing espionage under international law, since most cyber operations conducted today are espionage operations and not uses of force. Indeed, since the issue of the legality of espionage through the Internet is of much debate lately, the next section will review international legal principles relevant to that debate.

With respect to international organizations, there has been much discussion about the International Telecommunication Union (ITU) and its attempts to control the Internet by expanding its original mandate to cover international governance issues. Currently, states are in the midst of a debate about the most appropriate international venue to manage the Internet, and in particular, to establish and enforce the "rules of the road" for behavior on the Internet. States could pursue multiple options for establishing an institutional regime to build consensus on the "rules of the road" for behavior on the Internet. Such arrangements could entail efforts directly under UN auspices (the Security Council); the UN General Assembly (UNGA); or drafting individual treaties in the context of existing institutions such as the ITU, the Organisation for Economic Co-operation and Development (OECD), the International Civil Aviation

Organization (ICAO), or the World Intellectual Property Organization (WIPO). Although not the subject of this article, the designation of a specific international organization to ultimately play a central role in this area of international law will have implications not only for state sovereignty but for the development of international law related to national security issues such as espionage and conflict.

ESPIONAGE AS INFORMATION COLLECTION

Espionage, as the collection of intelligence, is a customary practice of states and is regarded as a vital necessity for national security. States collect intelligence to deter or minimize the likelihood of surprise attack; to facilitate defensive diplomatic, economic, and military action in the event of hostilities; and, in times of "neither peace nor war," to deter or defend against actions by individuals, groups, or nations that constitute a threat to international peace and security. Intelligence collection, as information gathering, is a continuous process in peace and war, although emphasis regarding sought-after information will vary depending on need and available assets. Espionage is the international norm. It may be denied or not admitted for diplomatic reasons, but efforts generally remain unacknowledged to prevent the denial of future intelligence.

Espionage, as intelligence collection, does not violate international law. However, some aspects of international law affect the means utilized in collection. For example, each state has the legal authority to control access to its territory and therefore criminalize espionage within its territory. The domestic prosecution of spies and domestic criminal laws enacted to do so constitute a form of denial of information rather than assertion of a violation of international law per se. These laws in no manner inhibit that state's efforts to collect intelligence about other states. No serious proposal ever has been made within the international community to prohibit intelligence collection as a matter of international law because of the tacit acknowledgement by states that it is important to all, and practiced by each.

PEACETIME ESPIONAGE/STUXNET:
AN ACT OF INTERVENTION?

Some may view Stuxnet as a series of unarmed interventions analogous to espionage under international law. Both unarmed interventions and espionage are forms of indirect or subversive intervention involving secret activity, as opposed to direct or open intervention such as an armed invasion. For those who may analyze Stuxnet as an unarmed intervention, it would be useful to review the relevant international rules related to such activity. Intervention is generally understood under international law to be actions that do not rise to the level of use of force but are still considered violations of international obligations. It follows that intervention in the cyber domain is cyber activities below the level of a "use of force" for purposes of the UN Charter prohibition on the use of force in Article 2(4). However, depending on the type of intervention at issue, intervention can rise to the level of a use of force.

International law is remarkably silent on the topic of peacetime espionage. Despite the widespread practice of peacetime espionage, it is a clandestine activity in which a commissioning state ordinarily has no visible or explicit contact with the target state. The debate over state-sponsored espionage centers on the question of whether espionage is prohibited by international law. Certainly, it would seem that the act of spying against other nations, whether through human assets or electronic surveillance, is of doubtful compatibility with the requirements of laws governing peaceful relations between states and the norm of nonintervention. Although not explicitly incorporated in the UN Charter, the norm of nonintervention is implied in Article 2(1) in the principle of sovereign equality of all states. As determined by the ICJ, the central fact in assessing whether something is an act of intervention under international law and therefore illegal is whether the action under question "uses methods of coercion."[5] Not all types of interference violate the law against nonintervention. Under the norm of nonintervention, as interpreted by the ICJ, cyber espionage that lacks a coercive aspect does not per se violate the nonintervention principle. Therefore, not all types of interference through the Internet would violate the law against nonintervention.

BEYOND ESPIONAGE: STUXNET, AN ACT OF INTERVENTION?

The basic principle of international law is the respect of each sovereign state for the territorial integrity and political independence of others. This long-established principle is accepted in the UN Charter based on the "sovereign equality of all its members."[6] The principle of nonintervention is mentioned in a number of treaties and UN resolutions, including the Declaration on Principles of International Law Concerning Friendly Relations and Co-operation among States in Accordance with the Charter of the United Nations. The United States has always accepted this principle, asserting it in the *Convention on Rights and Duties of States* (also known as the *Montevideo Convention*, 1933).[7] It is clear that intervention, defined as dictatorial interference in the internal or external affairs of another state, cannot be reconciled with the basic principles of international law. Intervention violates the territorial integrity and denies the political independence of another state.

In the definition of intervention, the focus is on dictatorial interference. While persuasion is said to be legitimate, coercion is illegitimate. While military invasion is considered coercive, what about economic embargo, secret infiltration, or incitement to subversion through propaganda? While it is difficult to distinguish dictatorial interference from proper influence, it is even more difficult to distinguish the internal affairs and foreign policy of a state from acts or utterances which so affect the rights and interests of another state that they can be regarded as issues of international concern, and as justifying interference—even dictatorial interference—by the affected state. In the *Nicaragua v. United States of America* case, the International Court of Justice held that supplying funds to insurgents was "undoubtedly an act of intervention in the internal affairs of Nicaragua," although not a use of force.[8] Mere intrusion into another state's systems does not violate the nonintervention principle.

However, if one accepts that Stuxnet went beyond the mere collection of information, which it did, then one needs to look closer at what international law defines as "intervention." Regarding the content of the principle, the court assessed that the principle prohibits coercive intervention with regard to matters on which each state is permitted to decide freely, including choice of political, economic, social, and cultural systems and the formulation of foreign policy. The language of the Declaration on Friendly Relations and the court's decision is broad enough to cover interventions by means of cyber operations when they have a coercive purpose; for example, when aimed at coercing a state into doing or not doing something that the state is otherwise legally entitled to do. But if the (nonforcible) intervention is a reaction against something the target state is not legally entitled to do (i.e., a breach of international law), then it could amount to a lawful countermeasure aimed at persuading the wrongdoing state to stop the breach and provide reparations. From this perspective, if Iran's nuclear program is an internationally wrongful act in the form of a violation of the Treaty on the Non-Proliferation of Nuclear Weapons and UNSC resolutions, the state conducting the countermeasure would be acting lawfully as long as the other elements of legal countermeasures were followed (see below for the discussion of countermeasures).

JUSTIFYING INTERVENTION OR USE OF FORCE FOR WRONGDOING: COUNTERMEASURES

A state can undoubtedly protest acts it deems violations of its rights and can make representations or even resort to economic retorsions (unfriendly but legal actions) against acts it deems adverse to its interests. It can go further and conduct reprisals not involving the use of armed force to rectify injuries arising from the violation of its rights, if the available peaceful means of adjustment or reparation have been exhausted without results and the means of reprisal are no more serious than the injury complained of. Ultimately, a state can resort to armed force to defend its territory or armed forces against armed attack, and to assist others who are victims of such attack.

But difficulties in establishing precise definition arise, especially in cyberspace. Can a state initiate reprisals on the basis of its own judgment that it has suffered from a breach of international law? Can a state carry out countermeasures against another state for violations of UNSC resolutions? How can it be determined if reprisal measures are in fact designed to rectify wrongs? What determines when peaceful remedies have been exhausted? Can defensive measures be taken preventively in case of immediate threat of invasion? These questions raise issues requiring careful analysis if the broad principles of international law are to be applicable in practice.

The debate about actions a state may take if victim of an international wrong centers on the international legal principle of countermeasures, or measures a state can lawfully take in recourse for a wrong done by another state either against the acting state or against the international community. So, in cases where a state has conducted a wrongful act in violation of international law (i.e., a breach of an international treaty obligation, an act of intervention, or a use of force), what can the victim state legally do in order to stop the wrongdoing of the perpetrator state? If the wrongful act does not rise to the level of an armed attack, states would not have the legal authority to use force in accordance with Article 51 of the UN Charter.

The customary international law of countermeasures governs how states may respond to violations of international law that do not rise to the level of an armed attack justifying self-defense. The Draft Articles on Responsibility of States for Internationally Wrongful Acts define countermeasures as "measures that would otherwise be contrary to the international obligations of an injured State *vis-à-vis* the responsible State, if they were not taken by the former in response to an internationally wrongful act by the latter in order to procure cessation and reparation."[9] Countermeasures are understood to mean necessary and proportionate actions that a state takes in response to a violation of international law by an offending state. It is generally accepted that for wrongdoings creating obligations owed to a group of states, one state can use countermeasures on behalf of other states whose rights were also violated by the offending state. While international law has not provided a list of acceptable countermeasures, and state practice is not fully in accord, it has begun to provide an outline of the parameters of acceptable behavior in carrying out countermeasures:

- First, countermeasures must be used in order to induce the offending state to comply with international law.
- Second, the state conducting the countermeasure must show that either it has been injured or it is acting on behalf of the international community that has suffered an injury because of the violator's actions.
- Third, before using countermeasures, the state must call upon the offending state to comply with international law, except when urgency is required in order to stop the injury from taking place.
- Fourth, the use of countermeasures must stop once the offending state complies with its obligations.
- And lastly, all countermeasures must be proportionate to the international wrong or injury suffered and targeted to the violator and not others.

There is dispute, however, over whether or not forcible countermeasures are allowed that would otherwise violate the Article 2(4) prohibition in the UN Charter. In a dissenting opinion by Judge Simma in the *Oil Platforms* (*Islamic Republic of Iran v. United States of America*) case, he argued that proportionate countermeasures could involve a limited degree of military force in response to circumstances below the Article 51 threshold of "armed attack."[10] In short, as long as the countermeasure did not rise to the level of an armed attack and was only a use of force, then the countermeasure could entail a certain limited level of force. Therefore, in the case of Stuxnet, one could argue that the state's action in launching Stuxnet against the illegal uranium enrichment facility in Iran was a lawful, forcible countermeasure.

PEACETIME ESPIONAGE/STUXNET: AN ACT OF AGGRESSION OR USE OF FORCE?

State practice, itself a major source of customary international law, seems to permit much of what would go into electronic surveillance through the Internet. Historically, all states have conducted espionage against adversaries and allies alike. Such intelligence collection activities typically take the form of sending intelligence officers undercover into another state's territory without that state's authorization in order to collect intelligence information and recruit foreign assets. Similarly, the practice of intercepting foreign telecommunications is well-established in international practice. In the UK, for example, the interception of "international telegrams" by government agencies has been authorized ever since Section 4 of the Official Secrets Act of 1920 empowered the Secretary of State to issue warrants for this purpose when he considered it "expedient in the public interest."[11] In the United States, the National Security Act of 1945 authorized the director of Central Intelligence to collect and analyze foreign intelligence information. Espionage, although universally criminal under domestic laws, does not by itself violate international law. Additionally, orbital remote sensing, which may include bombardment of a country's territory with radar or other forms of electromagnetic radiation, is permissible during times of war or peace.

It was the US sponsorship of the U-2 overflights of Soviet territory to obtain aerial photographs of military targets that led to a resurgence of interest in and concern about the international legal implications of espionage. In that case, the United States broke the old rules of the game by explicitly defending its recourse to espionage before the UNSC. On May 1, 1960, the US U-2 plane piloted by Francis G. Powers came down within Soviet territory. For the first time, a state acknowledged the fact that it was conducting intelligence operations within another state's sovereign airspace. The Soviet Union requested the UNSC consider this "Aggressive action by the Air Force of the United States of America against the Soviet Union."[12] The Soviet Foreign Minister Andrei Gromyko argued that since one plane can carry an atomic weapon, such an act justifies military retaliation.

The US Ambassador Henry Cabot Lodge denied that the United States had committed any aggressive action against the Soviet Union. Ultimately, the UNSC acknowledged that the US flights into Soviet territory did violate Soviet sovereign territory. However, all member states of the Security Council, except the Polish and Soviet representatives, refused to agree that the US U-2 flight constituted "aggression." In rejecting the Soviet resolution, the UNSC passed a resolution encouraging all states to "refrain from uses of or threats of force and to respect each other's sovereignty, territorial integrity and political independence."[13] The resolution affirmed the UN Charter principles codified in Article 2(4).

At the time, the United States argued its actions were lawful based on the Soviet Union's extensive use of espionage by sea, on land, and by hiring US aviators to take pictures of US strategic places. This argument by the United States, *tu quoque*, is based on the equitable principle that "he who seeks equity must do equity" that has been upheld by the ICJ. The UNSC seems to have given weight to this defense in rejecting the resolution proposed by the Soviet Union. Although the United States did not assert any equivalent cases of Soviet aerial surveillance, only arguing that the Soviets had used ships and agents for its surveillance against the United States, the UNSC still supported the United States and rejected the Soviet request for a resolution declaring the US action an act of aggression.

While in principle all peacetime espionage in foreign territory violates the sovereignty of the territorial state, it seems unreasonable to single out one state for utilizing a particular form of espionage when all are engaging in it, even though that mode of espionage (a U-2 plane that could possibly have been armed) carries possibilities of hostile action beyond espionage. Espionage is espionage and the variances in type should not dictate legality. Just as a U-2 plane can carry a bomb, a human asset can carry a bomb and computer software can be designed to carry an explosive payload. However, as the UNSC ruling in the U-2 incident reflects, if both parties are conducting espionage, whether the method is equivalent or not, it would be unreasonable under the law to find only one party in violation of the law.

Although the United States acceded to Soviet demands to terminate the U-2 flights, it also made public its program to achieve the same results by orbiting reconnaissance satellites over Soviet territory.[14] Two members of the Security Council, the Republic of China and Italy, noted that in view of the flights of man-made satellites and their potential for observation, air sovereignty had become more or less a myth. Similarly, the Internet has likely made state sovereignty in the cyber realm more a myth than a reality.

In the case of the US U-2 flight, both the Soviet Union and the United States assumed that aggression meant the use of armed force in international relations with aggressive intent. But they disagreed as to whether the penetration of foreign territory by an unarmed reconnaissance plane operating under government authority could be regarded as such a use of armed force. Based on the UNSC's decision in the case, the penetration and reconnaissance of an unarmed plane is not an act of aggression as the term is used for purposes of the UN Charter and its prohibition on the use of force. Likewise, since the penetration of foreign airspace by the U-2 for intelligence-gathering purposes was not regarded as a violation of the UN Charter, the utilization of cyberspace for similar purposes can be viewed as consistent with the purposes and intentions of the UN Charter and customary international law.

An act of aggression involves the actual use or threat to use armed force, forbidden by Article 2(4); an international breach of the peace or threat to the peace referred to in Article 39; or an "armed attack" justifying individual or collective self-defense under Article 51. Although states such as the Soviet Union have argued for the inclusion of a wider range of acts such as hostile propaganda and subversion in the concept of aggression, the predominate opinion confines the term to direct uses of, or threats to use, armed force with aggressive intent. This concept was assumed by a majority of the members of the UNSC in rejecting the Soviet Union's draft resolution by a vote of seven to two.

Notably, the United States has been in disagreement with the *Nicaragua* court ruling on the issue of what constitutes a use of force versus an armed attack. In that case, the court ruling distinguished the "most grave" form of the use of force (an armed attack) from other less-grave forms. The court held that the arming and training of armed opposition forces could constitute a use of force but the supply of funds could not. Both types of support could amount to unlawful intervention. It follows that all armed attacks would constitute uses of force but not all uses of force reach the threshold of an armed attack. The United States has disagreed with the ruling on this issue since the decision of the court. Recently, Harold Koh, in a speech at Cyber Command, upheld the US interpretation of a use of force versus an armed attack. He reiterated the US position is that any illegal use of force can qualify as an armed attack triggering the right of self-defense, thereby eliminating any gravity threshold distinguishing illegal uses of force from armed attack. This author believes that given the special circumstances the United States faces in the cyber domain, the United States may reconsider its position on this legal interpretation.

The court in both the *Nicaragua* case and the *Legality of the Threat or Use of Nuclear Weapons* advisory opinion also considered the meaning of the "threat to use force" in Article 2(4), but offered little specific guidance on this question. The concrete question it considered relevant for analysis of the Stuxnet case was: could the possession of nuclear weapons be a threat of force? In the *Nuclear Weapons* opinion, the court did provide a little detail on the question. It held that if the use of force envisaged was unlawful, a stated readiness to use it would constitute a threat prohibited under Article 2(4).[15] In the case of Iran's nuclear program, this analysis is relevant to the extent one argues that Iran's progress is a threat to use force in violation of Article 2(4). In this case, the legal options against this threat would be circumscribed by the principles of countermeasures that would be lawful against Iran.

It is generally accepted under international law that in assessing whether something is a use of force for the purposes of Article 2(4), one must look at the effects of the actions in the specific circumstances. If those effects reach the level of "gravity" illustrated in the *Nicaragua* case, then the actions would constitute a use of force. Stuxnet, arguably, was a use of force against Iran. Notably, however, under international law, the mere fact that a use of force has occurred does not authorize the victim state to use force in self-defense. States that have suffered or are facing a use of force that is not an armed attack cannot resort to a use of force in self-defense. The victim state that wants to respond lawfully would need to resort to countermeasures or actions that would be consistent with the plea of necessity. Only if there is an armed attack can a victim state use force in self-defense.

RIGHT OF SELF-DEFENSE: WHAT IS AN "ARMED ATTACK"?

According to the UN Charter and international customary law, even during a time of peace, each state maintains the inherent right of self-defense against ongoing or imminent armed attacks. According to Article 51 of the UN Charter, if a state suffers an armed attack, the victim state may use forcible measures of self-defense in order to stop or prevent the ongoing attacks. The victim state is free to choose the method it will use in self-defense (cyber or kinetic) as long as that forcible action is proportionate and necessary. So a state may lawfully act in self-defense outside of a war. Under international law, there are certainly challenges in characterizing which actions meet the threshold of "armed attack" for purposes of Article 51 of the UN Charter.

The UN Charter's prohibition against the use of force or acts of aggression is qualified by this limited grant of Article 51 that preserves "the inherent right of individual or collective self-defence if an armed attack occurs."[16] This notion of armed attack has to do with whether the target state may respond to an act with a use of force without itself violating the prohibition on using force. In the *Nicaragua* case, the ICJ used a "scale and effects" test as the criterion to distinguish actions qualifying as an armed attack from those that did not. The court noted the need "to distinguish the most grave forms of the use of force (those constituting an armed attack) from other less grave forms."[17]

THE GRAVITY TEST: ARMED ATTACK

The court established a "gravity" test for determining whether there was an "armed attack" or something lesser, like an intervention or a use of force, which may be unlawful but not an armed attack. The court clearly drew a distinction in the case between state actions that were armed attacks versus "mere frontier incidents." The court, however, gave no further guidance, leaving the parameters for an "armed attack" unsettled. The only element that the court dictated is that qualifying actions must be a use of force that is "grave." This part of the decision regarding the gravity test has been much criticized. Some, like the United States, have argued that it actually encourages the use of force (see the discussion above related to Harold Koh's speech about cyber operations and the US rejection of the court's gravity test). However, the court has not been swayed by the criticisms and upheld its gravity test in the *Oil Platforms* case.

The United States argued in the *Oil Platforms* case for an accumulation of events theory positing that a series of minor attacks that did not individually amount to an armed attack could cumulatively constitute an armed attack. The court was not swayed by this argument. Furthermore, in a separate opinion, Judge Simma rejected the doctrine, arguing that there was no "qualitative jump" from iterative actions below the threshold of Article 51 to those actions that would constitute armed attack as envisioned by the court.[18]

In all of the self-defense cases the court has considered (*Nicaragua, Oil Platforms, Democratic Republic of the Congo v. Uganda*, and the opinions in *Nuclear Weapons* and *Legal Consequences of the Construction of a Wall in the Occupied Palestinian Territory*), the court ruled that there was no "armed attack." In all of these cases, claims that there had been an armed attack were problematic because none of them included a classic cross-border action by the regular armed forces of an aggressor state. Especially in the context of cyber operations, based on the rulings in these cases, it would be unlikely that the court would find such an "armed attack" where cyber operations fall outside of traditional cross-border action by the regular armed forces of a state.

Internationally, legal scholars generally accept that those actions that cause injury or death to individuals would qualify as an armed attack. The majority of scholars also agree that those actions that cause damage or destruction would also qualify. Traditionally, espionage and theft would not qualify. It follows that in the cyber domain,

cyber espionage and cyber theft would not constitute an armed attack. Furthermore, actions that only temporarily incapacitate a system
(versus destroying or permanently damaging it) would not constitute
an armed attack. Under an effects- or consequences-based test, what
counts is not the specific type of weapon used but the end product
of its delivery to a selected objective. Scholars, however, have disagreed on what those effects are, based on whether one takes a broad
or more narrow approach related to types of effects under the test.
This author has argued that a useful test for the purposes of analyzing
whether an action rises to the level of an armed attack is offered by
one of the framers of the UN Charter in developing the criteria for
when the laws of armed conflict would be triggered (when an armed
conflict exists): scope, duration, and intensity.

Furthermore, in the *Nicaragua* case, the court had to decide
whether attacks by "irregular forces" could be regarded as armed attacks by a state, justifying the use of force in self-defense against another state. The court relied on the *Definition of Aggression* Article 3(g)
as applicable to this question. It ruled that attacks by irregular forces
could be imputable to states when there was "a sending by or on behalf of a state or armed bands. . .which carry out acts of armed force
against another state of such gravity as to amount to . . .an actual
armed attack conducted by regular forces, or its substantial involvement therein."[19] The court reaffirmed its position on this issue in the
Uganda decision. Today, much controversy centers on this part of the
decision in light of the September 11, 2001 terrorist attacks and the
role of nonstate actors.

This part of the decision will likely be particularly relevant in the
cyber context, where numerous nonstate actors have the capability
to launch destructive cyber operations. Many of these groups will
also be funded by or working on behalf of state actors. Unless there
is a direct link between the nonstate actors and the state, according
to the court, the right to execute self-defensive actions against the
nonstate actors within another state's territory (without UNSC authorization) will be doubtful. Clearly, detailed knowledge about the
nonstate actors and their relationship with the territorial state will be
critical to any legal justification to use force in self-defense. As with

the justification to use anticipatory self-defense, the credibility of the defense to use force will depend heavily on intelligence information gathered about the actors and the state supporting those actors.

NECESSITY AND PROPORTIONALITY REQUIREMENTS FOR SELF-DEFENSE

In addition to the UN Charter, the *Nicaragua* court pointed out that to determine what constitutes appropriate self-defense, one must also look to customary international law outlining the right of states to survive within the international community. Customary international law has established two key principles: proportionality and necessity. In state practice, these two requirements play a crucial role. Indeed, the ICJ has applied these two criteria in all of its use of force cases. It is certain that in any case of cyber operations, any legal analysis must also incorporate these two requirements into the assessment of the operation.

A state meets the requirement of necessity when it is evident that there were no other nonforcible options for stopping the threat. Timing will likely be important in the context of necessity. For example, if the use of force in self-defense was conducted after the threat had either diminished to the point where it no longer reached the level of an "armed attack" or had completely disappeared, the necessity of a self-defense action would also go away. In the context of Stuxnet, if one argues for a legal justification to use force in self-defense because Iran's actions constituted an "armed attack" (a difficult argument to make), then one would need to articulate that the threat of an "imminent" armed attack by Iran had not gone away at the time of Stuxnet's launch and that there were no other nonforcible means to stop the threat (i.e., sanctions).

In the alternative, if one argues that Iran's nuclear program is a "threat to use force" (an argument this author would support), then any "forcible" countermeasures (Stuxnet) in response to the wrongful actions of Iran would have to meet the requirement of necessity by showing that only "forcible" countermeasures are available to stop Iran's illegal activity (i.e., sanctions would be ineffective). Any countermeasures would have to stop once the threat had ceased to exist. Some might argue that once negotiations began with Iran to get Iran to stop its program, any forcible countermeasures would have needed to stop. Another potential position could be that as long as Iran continues to have a uranium enrichment program and denies the International Atomic Energy Administration (IAEA) access to the relevant sites, the threat continues and legal countermeasures could continue.

Proportionality requires that a state limit self-defense actions to the amount of force required to defeat an ongoing attack or to deter an imminent attack. Excessive force is prohibited. Three factors to consider in assessing the proportionality of self-defense are: size, duration, and the target of the forcible self-defense actions. The ICJ in the *Oil Platforms, Nicaragua,* and *Uganda* cases looked to these three factors in assessing the proportionality requirement for self-defense. In sum, any forcible action in self-defense will need to be tailored to the actual threat. It will matter where the actual self-defense actions are targeted. One must take into consideration the risks that would be inherent to innocent third parties when assessing the proportionality of the self-defense actions.

Assessing the proportionality and necessity of the victim state's actions in self-defense is at times difficult. Since the UN Charter does not define "armed attack" and the requirements of necessity and proportionality stem from custom and not treaty, definitional challenges have existed since the UN Charter was drafted. However, through UNSC resolutions, UN General Assembly resolutions, and ICJ decisions and opinions, terms like "use of force," "armed attack," and "aggression," as well as the principles of necessity and proportionality, have been construed to represent certain things.

ANTICIPATORY SELF-DEFENSE

Some argue that the language of Article 51 provides for a right of self-defense only in response to an actual armed attack. However, it has been the consistent position of successive US government administrations over many years that the right of self-defense under international law includes the right to use force when an armed attack is imminent. Under the criteria of the *Caroline* affair, anticipatory self-defense is lawful when there is an imminent attack, which is overwhelming, with no time for deliberations and no other means to resolve the issue. Other states have also supported this position, including the UK and Israel. This position is supported by the records of the international conference at which the UN Charter was drawn up and by state practice since 1945. The ICJ has never ruled on this issue. The UNSC, while not ruling directly on the issue, has given support to the principle in its ruling against Israel in the strike against the Osirak reactor in 1981. In that case, Israel argued its action was lawful based on anticipatory self-defense. The UNSC disagreed, finding that Israel failed to meet the criteria of self-defense based on the facts of the case. Certainly, the challenges North Korea and Iran have posed to the nonproliferation of nuclear weapons have expanded this question to whether the use of force might be justified in preventing certain states from acquiring nuclear weapons.

The majority of the international community supports the view that international law permits the use of force in self-defense against an imminent attack but does not authorize the use of force to mount a preemptive strike against a more remote threat. However, those rules must be applied in the context of the particular facts of each case. The concept of what constitutes an "imminent" armed attack under international law will develop to meet new circumstances and new threats. The concept of self-defense is not a static concept but rather one that must be reasonable and appropriate to the threats and circumstances of the day.

Based on the Bush administration's National Security Strategy of 2002, the US government concluded that the concept of "imminence" in anticipatory self-defense may require reassessment in light of the weapons of mass destruction threat. It was implied that the government should be very cautious to limit the application of the doctrine of anticipatory self-defense so as to prevent abuse by states pursuing their national interests.

CYBERWARFARE

There is no treaty that deals directly with the topic of cyberwarfare. The laws of armed conflict make no mention of cyber operations. Nor is it clear if there is any customary international law related to cyberwarfare, since state practice in the area of cyberwarfare and publicly available expressions of *opinio juris* are few. However, in the *Nuclear Weapons* advisory opinion, the ICJ affirmed that "the established principles and rules of humanitarian law…appl[y] to all forms of warfare, and to all kinds of weapons, those of the past, those of the present, and those of the future."[20] It is clear, however, that in a situation of ongoing kinetic hostilities amounting to an armed conflict, the applicable law of international or non-international armed conflict will govern cyber operations undertaken within that conflict.[21] So, for cyber operations that are part of an armed conflict, the rules related to international humanitarian laws and the laws of war, codified in the Geneva and Hague Conventions and in customary international law, will apply. However, as indicated by the very short mention of the laws of war in this article, most cyber activities to date involve actions that do not constitute "armed conflict."

THE FUTURE

The issues here are paramount for the future. In the cyber domain, cases of espionage or intervention without territorial intrusion are the very ones likely to be most vital for the future of humankind and the national security of states. With cyber capabilities, we are approaching a situation in which the reconnaissance function can be exercised without the traditional intrusion into state territory. If there is here an absence of any prohibition, what is left to consider is whether there should be a rule prohibiting such peacetime espionage or conflict in cyberspace.

This is a question of how the law should be changed or developed. Although arguments could be made in support of such a prohibition on espionage in cyberspace as well as against such a prohibition, limited space will not allow such arguments to be put forth here. The main point of this article is that if a state believes that cyber activities conducted by another state may constitute acts of intervention, use of force, or acts of aggression in violation of international law, any arguments in support of that position ought to be made before an impartial decisionmaker capable of making assessments based on interpretation of UN Charter provisions, past practice, and knowledge of state practice. The ICJ or the UNSC would be appropriate fora for discussions and appraisal of the legal arguments on both sides. Furthermore, in the absence of a specific set of facts referencing particular acts that have or are about to occur, the UNSC could decide that particular categories of cyber operations amount to a threat or breach to the peace, as it has done in the cases of international terrorism and the proliferation of weapons of mass destruction.[22]

Article 24 of the UN Charter gives the Security Council the primary responsibility for the maintenance of international peace and security and its decisions in this regard are binding on all members of the United Nations. Chapter VII, Article 39 of the UN Charter gives the UNSC the authority and responsibility to "determine the existence of any threat to the peace, breach of the peace, or act of aggression,"[23] and the UNSC can recommend and lead responses thereto.[24] To date, the UNSC has not determined that a cyber operation can constitute a threat to the peace, breach of the peace, or act of aggression. There is no dispute, however, over the UNSC's authority to do so. In addition, Article 41 of the UN Charter authorizes the UNSC to take measures to restore the peace, to include "complete or partial interruption of…postal, telegraphic, radio and other means of communication."

CONCLUSION

As the discussion of such terms as armed conflict, use of force, aggression, armed attack, and intervention has shown, it can be difficult to predict whether specific cyber operations will be considered to cross a specific legal threshold under international law. Certainly, state practice over the last two to three decades has indicated that states view the cyber domain as a legitimate realm for projecting state power and a means to achieve military and political objectives. Given this apparent reality, it is of utmost importance that states begin to agree on the terms of such activities in the cyber domain. As efforts through diplomatic channels continue through the UNGGE process and multiple bilateral discussions and Track II talks, there is an urgent need to begin to define the parameters of the specific international rules and thresholds discussed in this article as they apply to cyber operations.

Some take the view that the credibility of the law depends ultimately upon its ability to address effectively the realities of contemporary threats. Certainly, this is an accurate description of the implications for international law in the cyber domain. If states continue to operate in the cyber domain without any agreement on the boundaries and parameters of those actions, the law will begin to lose its legitimacy. The challenge is to formulate principles capable of attracting a broad measure of agreement that apply, or ought to apply, to the issues of intervention, use of force, and armed attack in cyberspace.

The most effective way to get some agreement on the rules of the road in cyberspace will be through state consent in some form, whether an international treaty, bilateral treaty, or nonbinding resolutions of one type or another. In an area of the law without many determinative decisions by the UN Security Council or the International Court of Justice, these agreements between states or the practice over time by states will likely be the manner in which international law on these issues will develop. Although a large number of cases directly or indirectly involving the use of force have been brought to the court, few have led to a judgment on the merits of international law on the use of force.

After the *Corfu Channel* case of the late 1940s, no cases on the use of force were decided on their merits until the *Nicaragua* case in 1986. The *Nicaragua* case is the most important decision by the court on the substantive law on the use of force. Importantly, however, it also raised issues about the court's role in cases concerning the use of force. In sum, the court is limited on matters related to questions of self-defense or aggression, given that the UN Charter has given a special role to the Security Council. These issues of the defined lines between the roles of the UNSC and the ICJ remain unresolved. However, given this tension and the court's unwillingness to make pronouncements on the legality of the use of force, it is very likely that these questions related to use of force, aggression, intervention, and self-defense will be answered by decisionmakers through their practice and, hopefully, agreements.

As a note of caution, however, waiting for custom to develop by state practice may not be the "safest" way for states to allow the law to develop. Although much more difficult, diplomatic efforts to get agreement among states would be much more preferable to allowing customary international law to develop over time, given that the United States is not the only actor, and may not be the primary actor in developing these customs.

One final word about customary international law, since there seems to be some misunderstanding among lay persons about its meaning and relevance under international law. First, customary international law, as a source of international law, is part of US domestic law. In other words, the United States should be interested in it not solely as a matter of international law but as a matter of US domestic law. Secondly, customary international law is based on the practice of states over a long period of time and *opinio juris*, the acknowledgement by states that they follow the practice according to the belief that it is a legal obligation. It is important to understand what one looks to in order to make claims about the existence of . The ICJ, in identifying *opinio juris*, has referenced UN General Assembly resolutions, statements by states, and agreements between states.

Why is this discussion of customary international law and *opinio juris* important in the context of Stuxnet, future cyber operations, and the development of international law? In the *Nicaragua* case, the court said that with regard to state practice on the prohibition on the use of force, absolute conformity with the rule was not necessary. It was sufficient that the practice of states in general was in conformity with the rule. The court went on to say that when a state violates the rule and defends its actions by appealing to exceptions or justifications contained within the rule, as opposed to saying nothing, for example, the result to is confirm rather than weaken that rule of international law. For cyber operations, where most activity will go unnoticed in general, it may be important for states like the United States to start to think about publicly acknowledging actions carried out such as Stuxnet accompanied by a justification or exception to the rule against force, thus making a legal argument publicly.

As the court highlighted, state actions alone are not sufficient in assessing state practice and the law. Additionally, the statements of states will play an important role in assessing the development of the law. The significance of cases of state conduct *prima facie* inconsistent with the principle of nonintervention or use of force lies in the nature of the grounds offered as justification. If a state's reliance on a new exception or justification of a rule of law were shared in principle by other states, then there could be a modification of customary international law. As the ICJ's judgments in use of force cases indicate, new rights to use force are not easy to establish.

In the case of Stuxnet, where there are probably grounds for justification, although too long to cover in this article, it may be in the self-interest of the United States and other states to articulate those grounds. These statements, however, cannot only be statements of international policy. In order to have an impact on the development of the law, the statements by a state must be an assertion of rules of existing international law. After Stuxnet, we must consider whether there are new rules emerging related to the circumstances of Iran's nuclear program and the use of cyber operations. Is there a new right of intervention or use of force emerging in the face of new threats and new technologies to combat those threats?

International law develops slowly and conservatively without radical deviation from already-established rules. For a new exception to a rule to develop, there must be state practice and *opinio juris* present. While changes to the law are possible, it is crucial that a state acting in that manner expressly claim a right to act in that manner. Inconsistent behavior by states would not help to form a new customary international law. It would be a breach of the existing law. This position is of great importance for contemporary debates on the use of force and how Iranian possession of nuclear weapons, the rise of nonstate actors and terrorists, and the development of cyberweapons have brought about changes in the law of self-defense.

Notes

1. Michelle Nichols, "Iran Says Terrorism Includes Any Attack on Nuclear Facility," Reuters, September 28, 2012, http://www.reuters.com/article/2012/09/28/un-assembly-nuclear-iran-idUSL1E8KS9IQ20120928.

2. United Nations, *Statute of the International Court of Justice*, April 18,1946, http://www.icj-cij.org/documents/?p1=4&p2=2.

3. Executive Office of the President of the United States, "International Strategy for Cyberspace: Prosperity, Security, and Openness in a Networked World," (Washington, DC, May 2011): 9, https://www.whitehouse.gov/sites/default/files/rss_viewer/international_strategy_for_cyberspace.pdf.

4. International Court of Justice, *Legality of the Threat or Use of Nuclear Weapons Advisory Opinion*, July 8, 1996, para. 39, http://www.icj-cij.org/docket/index.php?sum=498&code=unan&p1=3&p2=4&case=95&k=e1&p3=5.

5. International Court of Justice, *Case Concerning Military and Paramilitary Activities In and Against Nicaragua (Nicaragua v. United States of America); Merits*, June 27, 1986, para. 205, http://www.icj-cij.org/docket/?sum=367&p1=3&p2=3&case=70&p3=5.

6. United Nations, *Charter of the United Nations*, 1 UNTS XVI, entered into force October 24, 1945, Article 2(1), http://www.un.org/en/documents/charter/chapter1.shtml.

7. International Conference of American States, *Convention on the Rights and Duties of States (Montevideo Convention)*, December 26, 1933, Article 8, http://www.cfr.org/sovereignty/montevideo-convention-rights-duties-states/p15897.

8. International Court of Justice, *Nicaragua*, para. 228.

9. United Nations, "Draft Articles on Responsibility of States for Internationally Wrongful Acts, with Commentaries," commentary to chapter 2 (1), http://legal.un.org/ilc/texts/instruments/english/commentaries/9_6_2001.pdf.

10. International Court of Justice, *Case Concerning Oil Platforms (Islamic Republic of Iran v. United States of America)*, November 6, 2003, para. 64, http://www.icj-cij.org/docket/?sum=634&code=op&p1=3&p2=3&case=90&p3=5.

11. UK Parliament, "An Act to Amend the Official Secrets Act, 1911," December 23, 1920, 4(1), https://www.nsa.gov/public_info/_files/friedmanDocuments/ReportsandResearchNotes/FOLDER_057/41699569073890.pdf.

12. United Nations Review, June 1960, 1; July 1960, 6-7, 38-43.

13. United Nations Review, July 1960, 8-9, 48-50.

14. Ultimately, the right to conduct espionage in outer space was explicitly incorporated into the Strategic Arms Limitation Talks (SALT) II treaty (1979), which in Article 15

provides for the use of "national technical means"—generally understood to mean satellites and other means—for verification of compliance with the terms of the treaty. See https://history.state.gov/milestones/1953-1960/u2-incident.

15. International Court of Justice, *Nuclear Weapons.*

16. *Charter of the United Nations,* Article 51.

17. International Court of Justice, *Nicaragua,* para. 191.

18. International Court of Justice, Separate Opinion of Judge Simma, *Oil Platforms* case, http://www.icj-cij.org/docket/files/90/9735.pdf.

19. International Court of Justice, *Nicaragua,* para. 195.

20. International Court of Justice, *Nuclear Weapons,* para. 86.

21. The precise aspects of the law of armed conflict that apply depend on whether the conflict is international or non-international in character. The nature of the conflict is derived from the Geneva Conventions of 1949. International Committee of the Red Cross (ICRC), *Geneva Convention Relative to the Protection of Civilian Persons in Time of War (Fourth Geneva Convention),* August 12, 1949, 75 UNTS 287, Articles 2 and 3.

22. See e.g., United Nations Security Council Resolution 1373 (September 28, 2001); Security Council Resolution 1540 (April 28, 2004).

23. *Charter of the United Nations,* Article 39.

24. Ibid., Articles 41-49.

"US National Security Law after Stuxnet" by Merritt Baer

Stuxnet was a new incarnation of weapon. Because it was the first cyberattack to demonstrate kinetic effects, it elevated the significance of cyberattacks. It also brought them into the same dimension as other acts of war, to be governed by the same rules. In the United States, the national security laws Stuxnet may have triggered include international law of armed conflict, US national security law, and US computer criminal law. Stuxnet raised to the foreground the tensions present in our national security laws as developments in the cyber realm introduced new capabilities and challenged existing definitions. Stuxnet represents the need to reconstruct some of the rules surrounding legitimate use of force if we are to preserve the underlying values.

"Safety from external danger is the most powerful director of national conduct."

-Alexander Hamilton, *Federalist 8*

Stuxnet changed the conversation around US national security law because it demonstrated that the lines between the kinetic and the non-kinetic world are no longer distinct. It brought criminal computer law into the dimension of national security by dragging the stakes of computer crime into a context of kinetic violence.

Stuxnet was designed to target supervisory control and data acquisition (SCADA) computer systems, the systems that control electrical grids, transportation systems, and chemical processing plants. Stuxnet, a cyberweapon made of malicious code, exemplified the reality that "cyber" actions do not take place in an alternate universe, but in the same one we all inhabit. It was the first concrete herald of the fact that physical effects of "cyber" violence may be relatively unbounded—whether one hacked a hospital to produce lethal force or remotely accessed an urban traffic light system, there are physical ramifications of "cyber" violence. It broadened the realm of possibility for what kinds of laws might be triggered, and woke up the international community to the need to elaborate some codes of behavior in the cyber domain.

Of course, this resonates in the current controversy surrounding Edward Snowden's revelations. We expect some degree of protection from our laws, and we expect some degree of government sovereignty in executing its national security duties. Stuxnet showed blurred lines between use of force and foreign intelligence collection. The NSA's data collection blurs lines between national security law and basic civic protections.

In this paper, I present some of the relevant laws as applied to Stuxnet and discuss their significance in a post-Stuxnet world. National security law related to or triggered by Stuxnet falls broadly into three categories: US domestic law governing criminal computer use, US national security law, and international law governing armed conflict and use of force.

In many ways, Stuxnet was both an interesting case study and a harbinger of the forms of cyberattack that have emerged in ensuing years. It triggered formative questions around "just" cyberwar. Yet it is difficult to apply the national security legal structures that were written to create and maintain moral order in a world of kinetic violence to cyber actions. Stuxnet encapsulated the difficulty in drawing designations around cyber actions while retaining original commitments to verify legitimate use of force.

INTERNATIONAL LAW GOVERNING USE OF FORCE

International law has a number of laws surrounding use of force. They usually fall into the categories of why actors fight (*jus ad bellum*) and how actors fight (*jus in bello*). There are three basic principles in the law of war: 1) distinction, 2) proportionality, and 3) military necessity.

The United States has consistently maintained that international law applies equally to cyber actions and kinetic actions. This means that international humanitarian norms prescribing the limits and permissions afforded in armed conflict apply in a cyberattack.[1]

International law surrounding cyber conflicts was being developed long before Stuxnet was discovered in June 2010 and the attribution rumors confirmed by the *New York Times* in June 2012. Stuxnet was an accelerating force in developing the *Tallinn Manual on the International Law Applicable to Cyber Warfare*, a three-year project by an "independent group of experts" that attempts to apply the laws of war and international humanitarian law to cyberwarfare.[2] It is indisputable that Stuxnet contributed to the momentum to develop the *Tallinn Manual* (in addition to other significant publicized attacks, of course, such as the 2007 Estonia attacks that led the international community to house a cyber response center in Tallinn). But writing the rules is only the beginning of the conversation.

Without history or precedent upon which to hook determinations, we lack a metric for what proportionality and necessity mean in the context of cyber force, not to mention how we might measure—or even know—the extent of the targetedness. Moreover, recurring concerns around international law more generally may be amplified when it is applied to the cyber context. For instance, it may be even more difficult to impel adoption of protocols and treaties, and there are paramount questions regarding the enforceability of rules. Cyber also introduces the problem of attribution, because states must have airtight attribution to be able to properly punish infringers.

In March 2013, a group of North Atlantic Treaty Organization (NATO) researchers at the Cooperative Cyber Defense Center of Excellence in Tallinn determined that Stuxnet was an "act of force" and a likely violation of international law.[3] Earlier commentators had alleged that Stuxnet may have violated international law because it attacked a civilian target,[4] that it violated first strike proscriptions by extension, and that "a digital version of a US and Israeli military first strike makes the United States government and Israel civilly liable for the damage and disruption caused by Stuxnet."[5]

These findings were released to minimal fanfare and incited no reactive action. Stuxnet brought to the forefront questions of the force and reach of international law in cyberattacks, and those questions are far from answered.

US NATIONAL SECURITY LAW AND LAW OF ARMED CONFLICT

The enforcement mechanisms of US law are more tangible than international law. Rather than unenforceability, it appears that the United States' policy agenda means that the difficulty with applying cyber laws of armed conflict will stem from an unwillingness to declare criminality.

As Stuxnet demonstrated, a web of US national security laws might be applicable to cyberattacks, depending on the circumstances of the attack. Laws governing or invoked in response to cyber actions depend upon a number of factors, including the mode of information collection leading to the attack, the tools involved in the attack itself, the target, and the efficacy in hitting the target.

The relevant laws are grounded in constitutional concerns but include statutory and normative guidelines (which must comply constitutionally). Applying these to cyberattacks or "cyberwar"—a phrase often invoked but rarely meets any formal legal definition of war—presents difficulty. In particular, one of the most well-known and contentious statutes, the War Powers Resolution (1973), marked a sea change in national security law after Stuxnet.

WAR POWERS RESOLUTION

Cyberattacks challenge the statutory requirement that "the President in every possible instance shall consult with Congress before introducing United States Armed Forces into hostilities" because cyber offensives can be conducted without the appearance of traditional modes of force. How can we stipulate a requirement that the president submit to congressional oversight before extended military hostilities when we have not distinctly defined, and colloquial understandings do not clarify, what constitutes force or hostilities in the cyber realm?

Moreover, because the president may use force for up to sixty days without submitting it for congressional authorization, the law is not precise about whether the president needs authorization for a cyber program that takes months or years to develop but only finds hostile application for a short period of time. And we may conclude based on recent history that where lines around law of armed conflict are hazy, presidents are not shy about interpreting its scope to lend the broadest executive power.

But there is more: with the advent of drone warfare, it is clear that many, if not all, sophisticated weapons will have a cyber element. Again, Stuxnet emerges not only as the impetus for embracing a new understanding of US national security law but as a harbinger of a new, integrated model of warfare. Stuxnet introduced what can happen when cyber and kinetic tools are married to create both cyber and kinetic damage, blurring the lines of what requires congressional authorization.

This sea change led to the promulgation of Presidential Policy Directive 20 (PPD-20), signed in October 2012, which explicitly provides for Offensive Cyber Effects Operations (OCEO). The directive, which was secret but later leaked, claims that the OCEO can "advance US national objectives around the world with little or no warning to the adversary or target and with potential effects ranging from subtle to severely damaging."[6]

With these broad powers, it is clear that advances in cyber technology challenge existing national security definitions and result in an intensification of the president's power. As national security scholar and US Court of Appeals for the Armed Forces Chief Judge Jamie Baker observed back in 2007, "Definitions of 'national security' abound," but "the National Security Act does not define 'national security.' Neither does the PATRIOT Act."[7] Thus US national security law is driven by the politico–military situation in which the law is applied. It is unsurprising that it leads to potential overreach. The novel situations and the liberties the government has taken under espionage law are one other central area of national security law.

ESPIONAGE

Stuxnet began in earnest the conversation about the relationship of espionage to force in an age of sophisticated cyber tools. Espionage is, as many like to say, the second-oldest profession. But its current incarnation demonstrates that espionage can be closely related to the ways force is applied—indeed, it may be the invasion itself.

In the wake of Stuxnet, there was congressional debate about amending the Espionage Act to criminalize those who leaked information. Given the new stakes of cybersecurity, some lawmakers argued, we must be able to statutorily limit the information that becomes public. No prosecutions have been initiated as a result of Stuxnet, but there was speculation that cases would be brought against those who disclosed information about Stuxnet, including a four-star general and a set of journalists.[8] In the wake of the *New York Times'* publication of a leaked memo detailing President Obama's so-called terrorist "kill list," and even before the Snowden revelations, there was a sense of growing tension between the vast data collection the cyber domain enables and the open disclosure of that information.

Thus, Stuxnet raised questions about the collection of foreign intelligence and how far the government can and should go under the authorization of a set of hazy or evolving national security statutes. Snowden, of course, accelerated the legal conversation. While the Wiretap Act provides for a national security exception under which the foreign espionage at issue in Stuxnet could fall, the Foreign Intelligence Surveillance Act (FISA) was enacted in the 1970s specifically to provide another procedural safeguard against domestic surveillance. In the wake of September 11 terrorism concerns, these were augmented by the PATRIOT Act (2001) and then the FISA Amendment Act (2008; reauthorized in 2012), which allowed for broad domestic surveillance under the Business Records Exception, 50 U.S.C. Sec. 1861, and the General Acquisition and Interception Power, 50 U.S.C. Sec. 1881a. Stuxnet, unlike the Snowden revelations, involved foreign intelligence and not domestic, but formed an early example of what is now a momentous struggle to determine where to draw lines between openness and security. This struggle plays out not only in international but also in domestic surveillance and thus it has brought national security law to follow in the footsteps of US criminal computer law.

US CRIMINAL COMPUTER LAW

Stuxnet's malware contained instructions to do two things: cause Iranian centrifuges to destroy themselves, and prompt them to send messages back to the control center mistakenly indicating that they were operating properly.

These operations succeeded. But the weapon did not stop there. It continued on, destroying other equipment in what the national security law community terms "collateral damage." It spread to computers throughout a number of countries, including the United States.

In addition to Iran, Stuxnet is believed to have affected the functioning of SCADA systems in India, Pakistan, Bangladesh, Saudi Arabia, Canada, Russia, Kazakhstan, Belarus, Bahrain, Oman, Kuwait, the United Arab Emirates, Qatar, Brazil, Australia, Brunei, the Netherlands, China, Malaysia, South Korea, Taiwan, Indonesia, Myanmar, Thailand, the United Kingdom, Denmark, Germany, Finland, and the United States. New Zealand, Turkey, Japan, and Hong Kong issued alerts about Stuxnet's potential impact on their SCADA systems.

The Department of Homeland Security, for its part, released a series of alerts and bulletins through the Industrial Control System-Cyber Emergency Response Team (ICS-CERT), an interesting development since the United States government was identified as one of the parties involved in the development of Stuxnet in the first place.

Those warnings may have been necessary after all, even to the United States. Stuxnet showed that even the most tailored, sophisticated cyberweapons will result in unanticipated effects. Legal limits on behavior are thus complicated by the "Frankenstein's monster" threat, as it may be impossible for the developer or deployer of a cyberweapon to know all of the effects that will stem from the weapon's use.

In fact, Stuxnet may have violated federal US law because it went beyond its centrifuge target, resulting in damage to "federal interest" computers. The Computer Fraud and Abuse Act (CFAA), codified at 18 U.S.C. Sec. 1030, makes it criminal for anyone who "knowingly transmits a program, code or instruction, and as a result, intentionally causes damage, without authorization, to a protected computer."[9]

Speaking to an Australian audience, Eugene Kaspersky said in November 2013, "Unfortunately, the Internet doesn't have borders, and the attacks on very different systems somewhere far, far away from you in the very 'hot' areas of this world...they have the very same operating systems, the very same hardware."[10] He explicitly referenced Stuxnet, as after it completed its Iranian mission, it was allegedly discovered in the control station of a Russian nuclear power station and in the networks of the US oil company Chevron. The networks of affected private companies link Stuxnet to another key element of national security law after Stuxnet: we now recognize that national security in the cyber realm plays out on a landscape that includes private companies. Because private companies own most of the architecture of the Internet and actions take place within their bounds, it became clear after Stuxnet that private companies have a stake in the conflict. First, they will form the landscape on which the acts of espionage occur, and second, there is a likelihood that they will be affected by the downstream consequences of cyber offensives.

There are some existing laws of war for private, non-military companies that are not quite civilians by virtue of their actions or significance. These laws address the role of private military and security companies (PMSC); in other words, mercenaries engaged in war activity as a profession, not private telecommunications and Internet companies. Stuxnet demonstrated that a network battlefield can be both civilian and military at the same time, but the law does not adjust so readily. It is unsurprising, then, that we see questions about how private companies ought to figure into the national security law puzzle in the cyber domain. While many of the questions surrounding the laws of war are ancient and derive from long-established principles, there is no guide to address the tensions in the compulsory sharing of information under US national security justifications.

CONCLUSION

Stuxnet proved that conflict need not have the appearance of military force to invoke national security law. Cyber conflict involves actors that are not necessarily nation-states (though we have seen nonstate actors before in terrorism and organized crime around drugs).

Until 2010, cyber violence, cybercrime, and cyberwar were portrayed as cyber threats: occurring as solely cyber phenomena and incurring only cyber effects. As we come around to how *real* the Internet is, whether real bank accounts being hacked or real centrifuges being combusted, there has been a shift in understanding that we have fundamentally the same concerns online and the same need for rules governing conduct.

Stuxnet raised the stakes. But it also perpetuated doomsday fears. Stuxnet opened the door to talk about "kill switches" and "downing the grid" as though every system is equally and openly vulnerable. It is important to steer the post-Stuxnet conversation back to reality to avoid extremes in national security law permissiveness. While the stakes are high, the approaches are likely knowable and the vulnerabilities can certainly be better addressed. I urge us to address the world as it currently is when we come to cybersecurity, and to imagine a world in its best form as we formulate principles by which to live.

Notes

1. Executive Office of the President of the United States, "International Strategy for Cyberspace: Prosperity, Security, and Openness in a Networked World," (Washington, DC, May 2011), https://www.whitehouse.gov/sites/default/files/rss_viewer/international_strategy_for_cyberspace.pdf.

2. NATO Cooperative Cyber Defence Centre of Excellence, *Tallinn Manual on the International Law Applicable to Cyber Warfare*, ed. Michael N. Schmitt, (Cambridge: Cambridge University Press: 2013), http://www.ccdcoe.org/249.html.

3. Shaun Waterman, "US-Israeli Cyberattack on Iran was 'Act of Force,' NATO Study Found," *Washington Times*, March 24, 2013, http://www.washingtontimes.com/news/2013/mar/24/us-israeli-cyberattack-on-iran-was-act-of-force-na/?page=all.

4. See International Committee of the Red Cross (ICRC), *Geneva Convention Relative to the Protection of Civilian Persons in Time of War (Fourth Geneva Convention)*, August 12, 1949, 75 UNTS 287, Annex I, Articles 1-13; International Conferences (The

Hague), *Hague Convention (IV) Respecting the Laws and Customs of War on Land and Its Annex: Regulations Concerning the Laws and Customs of War on Land*, October 18, 1907, Articles 27-28, 54. See also the EastWest Institute, *Working Towards Rules For Governing Cyber Conflict,* (January 2011), 12.

5.   Wayne Madsen, "Stuxnet: A Violation of US Computer Security Law," *OpEdNews*, January 19, 2011, http://www.opednews.com/articles/Stuxnet-A-Violation-of-US-by-Wayne-Madsen-110119-734.html.

6.   Executive Office of the President of the United States, Presidential Policy Directive 20 (PPD-20), (Washington, DC, October 2012), http://www.theguardian.com/world/interactive/2013/jun/07/obama-cyber-directive-full-text.

7.   James E. Baker, *In the Common Defense: National Security Law for Perilous Times*, (Cambridge: Cambridge University Press, 2007): 16.

8.   Awr Hawkins, "Will White House Prosecute Four Star General as Stuxnet Leaker?," *Breitbart*, June 28, 2013, http://www.breitbart.com/Big-Peace/2013/06/28/Will-White-House-Prosecute-Four-Star-General-As-A-Leaker; and Annika McGinnis, "House May Prosecute Journalists for Reporting Leaked Information," *Christian Science Monitor*, July 11, 2012, http://www.csmonitor.com/USA/Latest-News-Wires/2012/0711/House-may-prosecute-journalists-for-reporting-leaked-information.

9.   US Department of Justice, Computer Crime and Intellectual Property Section, Criminal Division, *Prosecuting Computer Crimes*, (2nd ed., 2010), http://www.justice.gov/sites/default/files/criminal-ccips/legacy/2015/01/14/ccmanual.pdf.

10. Stilgherrian, "Cyber Espionage 'Extremely Dangerous' for International Trust: Kaspersky," *ZDNet*, November 7, 2013, http://www.zdnet.com/cyber-espionage-extremely-dangerous-for-international-trust-kaspersky-7000022915/.

"Stuxnet and the Internet Governance Debate: The Growing Convergence of Internet Policy Issues and Communities" by Merritt Baer and Tim Maurer

TWO THOUSAND TWELVE WAS AN important year in Internet history for at least two reasons.[1] First, on June 1, the *New York Times* published an article titled, "Obama Order Sped up Wave of Cyberattacks Against Iran."[2] The report identified the Stuxnet malware, which had been discovered two years earlier targeting an Iranian nuclear facility, as a covert program carried out by the US and Israeli governments code-named "Operation Olympic Games."[3] Second, the World Conference on International Telecommunications (WCIT) in December revealed a significant split in the international community about its views on the future of the Internet.[4] The conference ended in an éclat. Against previous statements that any conference outcome would be consensus-based, a vote took place. Only eighty-nine states ended up signing the new treaty while some fifty opposed it. This paper raises the question of whether the two were related, and specifically whether Stuxnet had an effect on the WCIT and the Internet governance policy debate.

Our analysis suggests that Stuxnet has had only a limited and indirect effect on international Internet governance policy discussions to date. We base this conclusion on three indicators. First, at the time of writing, a year after the WCIT and a year and a half after the *New York Times* article, we assume that media reports or academic articles would point to such a connection if it did exist. However, there is a paucity of literature suggesting Stuxnet had an impact on the Internet governance policy debate, in spite of the media attention both received separately.[5] Second, there is little evidence of governments referencing Stuxnet in Internet governance negotiations, which would have signaled a significant effect. Third, responses to a survey we sent to Internet policy experts from different countries, communities, and institutions gave further evidence of the tenuousness of the connection. The replies revealed similar assessments by experts across the globe, who opined that there was no significant effect of one upon the other, in line with our initial research.

While Stuxnet did not have a significant direct effect on the Internet governance policy debate, several indirect effects seemed to arise. First, the malware raised awareness among the Internet governance community of the rising security threats and concerns relating to cyberspace. For example, Internet governance scholar Milton Mueller, professor at Syracuse University, mentioned in his survey response that "making the public aware of the so-called 'Olympic Games' project affected the Internet governance debate…it made it clear that cyberweapons were real, and thus that militarization of the Internet and 'arms control' negotiations should play a role in Internet governance discussions." This view was also expressed by other respondents outlined below. One of the main lasting effects of Stuxnet therefore seems to be that it contributed to a convergence of the security and governance policy areas, and fostered awareness between the two distinct communities. Several respondents made the caveat though that Stuxnet's effect pales in comparison to what some termed "the Snowden effect."

In the following sections, we outline our research in greater detail. We discuss the existing literature addressing and surrounding

Stuxnet's impact on the Internet governance policy debate, specifically in the context of the WCIT in 2012. (It is important to note that the focus of this paper is on the Internet governance *policy* debate, especially on the process leading up to the WCIT and the sessions of the WCIT itself. There are many different ways to define Internet governance, including a focus on its technical dimension, which are beyond the scope of this paper.) We present the survey results, including a summary of the responses we received, and our interpretation thereof. In the next section, we outline further implications, followed by conclusions and key take-aways.

DETERMINING STUXNET'S EFFECT ON THE INTERNET GOVERNANCE DEBATE: A REVIEW OF THE LITERATURE COMPLEMENTED BY A SURVEY OF INTERNET POLICY EXPERTS

Several months after Stuxnet's discovery, another malware program called "Flame" attracted the attention of the security researcher community.[6] So before reviewing the literature on Stuxnet, we explored whether the two are related and whether Flame would also have to be included in our review. We found that Kaspersky Lab concluded in 2012 that "the source code of at least one module of Flame was used in Stuxnet," establishing a link between the two.[7] Our review of the literature therefore included both Stuxnet and Flame.

Our literature review on Stuxnet and Flame unearthed very few texts examining their effect on the Internet governance debate. Several publications published shortly after their discovery and before the WCIT mentioned a potential impact. Adam Segal at the Council on Foreign Relations, for example, wrote, "There is little risk of 'blowback,' but the United States will have to try harder to convince Brazil, India, and South Africa of the merits of the multistakeholder model."[8] And according to James Lewis at the Center for Strategic and International Studies, "Stuxnet should not surprise anyone. It along with Flame will likely be used by Russia and China for political effect."[9] However, there is a lack of literature on the issue <u>after</u> the WCIT took place in December 2012. This suggests that no significant effect was observed.

We therefore decided to complement our literature review with a survey specifically targeting Internet policy experts. The survey was based on our initial findings from the literature review suggesting that whether Stuxnet actually had a significant effect on the Internet governance debate remained an open empirical question. The questions were the following:

1. Did Stuxnet change the Internet [g]overnance debate in any significant way? If so, how?
2. Did Flame change the Internet [g]overnance debate in any significant way? If so, how?
3. Where could Internet governance efforts go in the next few years after Stuxnet and Flame?
4. Are you aware of any governments mentioning Stuxnet or Flame in Internet [g]overnance negotiations or making a link between them?
5. Please share any other related thoughts you might have.

The survey questions were deliberately written to be broad and open-ended as an independent test of our emerging hypothesis that Stuxnet (and Flame) had a limited impact on the Internet governance debate. The survey design prioritized quality over quantity, specifically targeting experts familiar with the topic. It was sent to a total of fifty experts with a 62 percent response rate (thirty-one responses) and 38 percent (nineteen responses) providing substantive feedback. The nineteen respondents providing substantive feedback come from ten countries representing six continents and two international bodies:

– Australia, Brazil, Canada, Germany, Japan, South Africa, South Korea, Switzerland, United Kingdom, United States
– International Telecommunication Union, ICANN

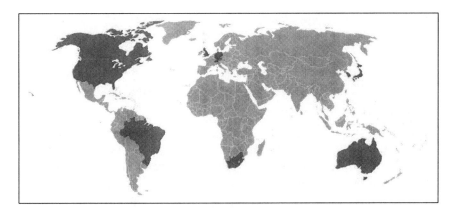

The survey responses supported our findings from the literature review. There was a general consensus among the respondents that neither Stuxnet nor Flame changed the Internet governance debate in any significant way. For example:

Alex Comninos, researcher for the Association for Progressive Communications, South Africa: "I don't think it changed Internet governance discourse in such a significant way. Issues such as Stuxnet fall under overlapping discourses of cybersecurity, but usually discussion is securitized such that issues such as Stuxnet are talked about by states, and not in multistakeholder contexts."

Dr. Rex Hughes, cybersecurity researcher at the University of Cambridge, United Kingdom: "I do not believe there is much hard evidence at present that shows Stuxnet or Flame having a major impact on mainstream Internet governance debates. While some countries and NGOs have called attention to both incidents in track I and II fora, I personally do not see much evidence of major policy impact and/or transfer to date."

William Drake, lecturer, University of Zurich, Switzerland: "It depends on what one considers to be 'the IG debate'; if one spends a lot of time in security-specialist circles where info war is a leading preoccupation, then I suppose the answer's obviously positive. But with regard to the mainstream, nonspecialist debates—e.g. in

ICANN, IGF, CSTD, ITU, etcetera—I cannot say I've detected a
notable impact of Stuxnet and Flame, now or even back in 2010."

There is also very limited evidence of governments mentioning
Stuxnet or Flame in Internet governance negotiations or making a
link between them.

Adam Peake, executive research fellow, Center for Global Communications, Japan: "I've seen very little mention of Stuxnet (Flame)
in any Internet governance discussions. I think people probably felt
it fell into the type of cyberwar/terrorism action expected from
governments."

Marilia Maciel, FGV Center for Technology and Society, Brazil: "I
am not aware of direct references, although it is hard to affirm for
sure."

Only one respondent—Yoko Nitta of Japan—was aware of any
governments mentioning Stuxnet or Flame in Internet governance
negotiations or making a link between them. She observed, "Russia plots to strip the US of its Internet governance, taking advantage
of the Stuxnet and Flame incidents. Russia tries to galvanize public
opinion and will try to transform the control over the Internet to
BRICS." She predicts that part of the fallout from Stuxnet will be
that, "Those countries which raised objections for some time against
[the] US such as Russia and China in terms of the concept of Internet governance, they will pursue their interest[s] like censoring
now that they c[an] justify their aim under the name of security and
national security."

Two respondents offered hypotheses to explain the lack of references. Hughes made the argument that there are also structural reasons for this observation: "From my perspective, Stuxnet and Flame
largely fall under covert espionage actions that are not yet governable
by international law and it is hard to see how the above attacks influence major Internet governance debates—i.e. how do you govern/
regulate something that does not officially exist?" The haziness of

jurisdiction is therefore one possible explanation for the dearth of literature. In general, there was a sense that Stuxnet and Flame stand for a process that has not yet been part of the Internet governance debate.

Maciel, on the other hand, points out that Stuxnet "practically showed the potential to use cyber attacks as complementary strategy not only to military attacks, but also for diplomatic discussions concerning peace and security. The worm was being used to halt or to delay the nuclear program while sanctions were being discussed in the UN Security Council. This cyberattack disregarded the authority of the Council, and it is interesting how countries were not vocal against this unilateral move, including Brazil, which had a direct interest in the Iranian issue because of the Turkish-Brazilian attempt to break an agreement." This suggests that states might have had other interests that explain why they did not make explicit references to Stuxnet.

The survey responses overall consisted of a range of feedback. Some interview subjects replied that Stuxnet and Flame had impacted Internet governance substantially; others could not summon more than a few sentences about its mootness. However, a closer look explains this variance, and we therefore distinguish between direct and indirect effects in this paper.

STUXNET AND FLAME HAD INDIRECT EFFECT BY BOLSTERING EXISTING ARGUMENTS

Sandro Gaycken, a cybersecurity researcher at the Freie Universität Berlin, Germany, pointed out, "in backdoor discussions [Stuxnet and Flame have been mentioned] a lot, but rather as exemplifications, not as unique cases."

Similarly, another expert who chose to remain anonymous asserted that some governments have used the malware as an example of why there is a need for a new Internet governance model, but pointed out that they had already been making such arguments without Stuxnet and Flame.

STUXNET AND FLAME HAD INDIRECT EFFECT BY UNDERMINING EXISTING ARGUMENTS

Greg Austin, a professorial fellow at the EastWest Institute, argued that Stuxnet undermined the existing narrative of the United States. In response to the question, "Did Stuxnet change the Internet governance debate in any significant way? If so, how?" he replied:

> Fundamentally. It completely undermined the position laid out by Secretary of State Clinton that states [that] do this should be regarded as outlaws. She used this language: 'Countries or individuals that engage in cyber attacks should face consequences and international condemnation. In an Internet-connected world, an attack on one nation's networks can be an attack on all.'... As I understand the two [Stuxnet and Flame], Stuxnet was notable for sabotage. Flame was/is espionage, without sabotage. Stuxnet was a clear breach of international law (sabotage across state borders in peacetime), whereas Flame was not such a clear breach of international law (as espionage).

STUXNET AND FLAME HAD INDIRECT EFFECT BY AFFECTING AGENDAS AND AWARENESS

Maciel: "Cybersecurity and defense were ranked higher on the agenda, both on the international and on the national levels."

Gaycken: Stuxnet "accelerated the security discussion and rendered security more important in this arena."

The following responses show such increased awareness:

Former Canadian Ambassador Paul Meyer: "Stuxnet did represent a certain crossing of the Rubicon in terms of a state-directed cyberattack with the aim of causing physical damage to a sensitive facility. This has great significance for governance in that it demonstrates the dangers of leaving this realm unregulated and should serve as an impetus for states to start developing some cooperative security arrangements…The implication for global governance lies in the practical necessity to delineate between cyberattacks and cyber exploitation…I am concerned that opportunities for preventive diplomacy are being missed while the militarization of cyberspace intensifies."

Mueller: "The US was inaccurately perceived (mostly in domestic circles, but also in some foreign circles) as a neutral steward that could protect the Internet against repressive control by states… Stuxnet/Flame got people thinking. NSA/Snowden sealed the deal." He added, "because Stuxnet relied on an exploit tied to Microsoft's update process, it raised concerns that the company might be cooperating with US military/intel agencies behind the scenes…and raised doubts about the role of US-based businesses."

Nitta: "[the] US…voice[d] that [the] Internet is for freedom and democracy, maintaining the values of free-flowing information fostering innovation and economic prosperity within Internet governance bodies[.] [H]owever, this shows the hypocrisy of [the] US that they use [the] Internet as their pursuit of political motivation taking advantage as its inventor.

Myriam Dunn Cavelty, senior researcher, ETH Zurich, Switzerland: "Security has become one of the prime 'goals' in the cyber debate, currently trumping other possible goals or focal points. The type of security that is upmost in people's minds is 'national' security. And national security has a tendency to come with a desire for control – and borders. And often, with the strengthening of military capabilities. It is likely that the so-called 'Balkanization of the Internet' is accelerating, that more and more states will favor national over international solutions. National solutions come with more state control of information flows (out and in) and a further 'territorialization' of the Internet. It is hard to see what exactly this process will lead to and what the consequences for us, the user[s], will be, not least because the processes will be diverse and fragmented and definitely not linear, affecting different people in different regions/countries in different ways. I expect much resistance by the technologically apt."

Several respondents replying to the question about where Internet governance efforts could go in the next few years after Stuxnet and Flame identified a trend of convergence between Internet governance and cybersecurity:

> Marco Obiso, cybersecurity coordinator, International Telecommunication Union (ITU): "There is [a] growing tendency to put under the same umbrella cybersecurity-related issues with the Internet governance debate, as well with human rights and freedom of expression."

> So Jeong Kim, senior researcher, Attached Institute of ETRI, South Korea: "I think every Internet governance-related meeting will focus on the CIIP [critical information infrastructure protection] in-depth for a while. It's because it has direct impact on the people's living and more advanced countries will be easier targets for the CIIP cyber attack with unpredictable results."

> Maciel: "There could be a stronger tendency of 'securitization' of the agenda. Securitization may alienate nongovernmental actors, [e]specially civil society, from the debate."

In short, while some respondents speculated that there might be fallout from Stuxnet that affected the Internet governance debate prior to the WCIT, the survey results provided further evidence that Stuxnet did not have a significant effect on the Internet governance policy debate. Some countries apparently referenced and used Stuxnet for political purposes in closed-door discussions but not in public debate and the WCIT negotiations. With regard to indirect effects, Stuxnet did raise awareness among the Internet governance policy community of the security dimension, and likely accelerated countries' efforts to gain domestic control over infrastructure. Russian scholar Elena Zinoviev describes how the events of the Arab Spring and the media reports of "Twitter revolutions" contributed to the state's desire to strengthen its sovereignty in the global information space. According to her, additional impetus came from Stuxnet demonstrating that cyberwarfare is not the abstract scenario but real international practice.[10]

IMPLICATIONS AND OUTLOOK

The kinetic effect of Stuxnet was a wake-up call to many. Stuxnet proved that it is possible to develop a highly sophisticated, tailored malware program, but that its consequences remain unpredictable. Its spread throughout the control systems connected to the Internet around the world demonstrated this and underlines the uncertainty about how interdependent systems really are. It demonstrated that the public underestimated cyber threats until the potential for physical effects became apparent—in spite of early evidence such as the video of a staged cyberattack leaked to CNN in 2007.[11] Stuxnet turned an experiment into reality. While some have made the connection between Stuxnet and the espionage that Snowden exposed, others see them as different spheres of action. This disconnect is exemplified by Meyer's remarks about the need to differentiate between cyber exfiltration and cyberattacks. Both forms of action reinforced international perceptions that the United States holds asymmetrical cyber power to the point of dominance, furthering concerns about the relationship between the US government and companies based in the United States and debates about the use of cyberspace for military purposes.

Stuxnet exemplified the asymmetry of cyber capabilities among countries and demonstrated that the major powers currently are more interested in conducting espionage and cyber aggression than in limiting it. Mueller argues that Stuxnet disabused the international community of the notion that the United States was a neutral guardian of Internet rights. It became apparent that the United States pursues, and is willing to use, military-grade technology in cyberspace.

Despite the US and other countries' agendas, there may be areas of cooperation, particularly focusing on the low end of malicious Internet activity (botnets, spam, financial crime, and fraud) and the high end (lethal attacks on civilians). For instance, there is significant international collaboration to tackle child pornography. On the other hand, there are reasons to be skeptical of the possibility of truly global cooperation. Nitta observed that function follows form and other "democracies are uncomfortable with China's model of Internet censorship but also suspicious of the US preference for a multistakeholder model of Internet governance."

As many interviewees noted, public reaction to mass surveillance revelations, or "the Snowden effect," has elicited a more distinct reaction and indeed eclipsed the reaction to Stuxnet. In some connected ways, however, the NSA leaks may have drawn to the foreground the need for effective Internet governance work. In Drake's words, "because of PRISM we're all going off to Sao Paulo [for first Global Multistakeholder Meeting on Internet Governance] in April to discuss—well, issues other than PRISM." The Snowden revelations have accelerated the convergence of communities according to cybersecurity expert James Lewis, speaking at the 2012 Seoul Conference on Cyberspace. Andrew Puddephatt, executive director of Global Partners Digital in the United Kingdom, summarized what other respondents repeated: "the NSA revelations have dwarfed everything else and will have the biggest impact on Internet governance."

CONCLUSION

This paper is not a peer-reviewed academic paper, but our preliminary review of the literature and survey suggest that our finding is quite robust. Stuxnet's effect on the Internet governance policy debate was limited and mostly indirect. At the same time, it is too early to assess Stuxnet's broader long-term consequences for the international system beyond the Internet governance policy debate. For example, Iran, the country targeted by Stuxnet, has seen significant changes in its national network infrastructure and governance from a technical perspective in recent years.[12] It is unclear what has been primarily driving these efforts, but two credible explanatory factors are the 2009 Green Movement and Stuxnet—most likely, both.

Austin's remarks suggest that Stuxnet might have had a broader effect on diplomacy beyond the Internet governance policy debate itself. Stuxnet was a wake-up call and raised awareness among the

Internet governance community of the security dimension. Arguably as a result of this growing awareness, several interviewees expressed a desire to see countries begin to build their diplomatic capabilities to match their military capabilities in cyberspace. Stuxnet has therefore likely had an indirect effect and contributed to a convergence of policy issues and communities. This link was explicitly mentioned at the Seoul Conference on Cyberspace and has also become part of draft resolutions on cybersecurity with references to Internet governance. It remains unclear how this increasing convergence will affect the discussions on both issues of security and governance.

Generally, the convergence of these issues and communities bears the potential for clashes in terms of both substance and process. While security negotiations remain firmly enshrined in traditional intergovernmental processes, the Internet governance debate has been institutionalized within the multistakeholder model since 2005 and is among the most inclusive global governance set-ups generally. This model was the result of a broader push by civil society organizations, especially during the 1990s, for more inclusivity at various summits organized by the United Nations.[13] In recent years, this dynamic has become embedded in the current systemic shifts in the international system: namely the establishment of the G20, changes to the voting structures of the International Monetary Fund (IMF), and calls for UN Security Council reform. And while the ITU leadership strategically positioned the organization in the emerging Internet policy debates, the debate over the organization's role has become highly politicized.

In short, the efforts to find agreement on how to govern the Internet are not only complicated by the unique features of the technology itself but aggravated by the significant fundamental changes to the global order that are currently taking place, remain in flux, and have yet to be institutionalized. There has also been a notable absence of a middle power playing the role of an honest broker accepted as such by the big powers, which could be a useful intermediary step to address some of the issues. Last but not least, the quest for a more inclusive institution perceived as legitimate is not limited to but particularly pronounced in the Internet policy realm due to the role of nongovernmental actors governing and operating much of the infrastructure.

Notes

1. A third important milestone in 2012, which is not the focus of this paper, was the resolution adopted by the UN Human Rights Council affirming that human rights must be protected online as well as offline. (United Nations General Assembly, Human Rights Council Twentieth Session, 20/L13… The Promotion, Protection and Enjoyment of Human Rights on the Internet, A/HRC/20/L.13 (June 29, 2012), Office of the High Commissioner for Human Rights website, http://www.loc.gov/lawweb/servlet/lloc_news?disp3_l205403231_text).

2. David E. Sanger, "Obama Order Sped Up Wave of Cyberattacks against Iran," *New York Times*, June 1, 2012, http://www.nytimes.com/2012/06/01/world/middleeast/obama-ordered-wave-of-cyberattacks-against-iran.html.

3. While the US government has not officially acknowledged the accuracy of the reporting, NBC News reported a year later that the former vice-chairman of the Joint Chiefs of Staff was under investigation by the Department of Justice for allegedly leaking information about the operation to the *New York Times*. "Ex-Pentagon General Target of Leak Investigation, Sources Say," NBC News, June 27, 2013, http://investigations.nbcnews.com/_news/2013/06/27/19174350-ex-pentagon-general-target-of-leak-investigation-sources-say.

4. For more details on WCIT, see Tim Maurer, "What's at Stake at WCIT?" *New America Foundation,* December 5, 2012, http://newamerica.net/publications/policy/whats_at_stake_at_wcit.

5. Please note that this assessment is based on a review of literature in English; texts in other languages might offer different conclusions.

6. For more details on Flame, see Tim Maurer and David Weinstein, "Flame Thrower," *Foreign Policy*, May 29, 2012, http://www.foreignpolicy.com/articles/2012/05/29/flame_thrower.

7. Kaspersky Lab, "Resource 207: Kaspersky Lab Research Proves that Stuxnet and Flame Developers are Connected," June 11, 2012, http://www.kaspersky.com/about/news/virus/2012/Resource_207_Kaspersky_Lab_Research_Proves_that_Stuxnet_and_Flame_Developers_are_Connected.

8. Adam Segal, "Stuxnet and Flame: Take a Breath," *The Diplomat*, June 7, 2012, http://thediplomat.com/flashpoints-blog/2012/06/07/stuxnet-and-flame-take-a-breath/.

9. James A. Lewis, "In Defense of Stuxnet," *Military and Strategic Affairs* 4, no. 3 (December 2012), http://i-hls.com/wp-content/uploads/2013/04/In-Defense-of-Stuxnet.pdf.

10. Elena Zinoviev, "Digital Westphalia," MGIMO, March 26, 2013, http://www.mgimo.ru/news/experts/document236588.phtml.

11.   Jeanne Meserve, "Sources: Staged Cyber Attack Reveals Vulnerability in Power Grid," *CNN News*, September 26, 2007, http://edition.cnn.com/2007/US/09/26/power. at.risk/.

12.   Daisy Carrington, "Iran Tightens Grip on Cyberspace with 'Halal Internet,'" *CNN News*, June 3, 2013, http://www.cnn.com/2013/06/03/world/meast/ iran-internet-restrictions-halal-internet/.

13.   See the World Summit on the Information Society website, http://www.itu.int/wsis/ basic/multistakeholder.html.

Foreign Reactions
to Stuxnet

"Russia's Response to the Stuxnet Incident" by Timothy Thomas[1]

INTRODUCTION

According to Sir Isaac Newton's third law of motion, for every action there is an opposite and equal reaction. The discovery of the Stuxnet virus elicited a host of reactions worldwide, as the mere thought of this virus first of all caused speculation and ended in both motion and commotion, as analysts and policymakers developed private and official responses.

Perhaps Russia's reaction to a Belarusian analyst's discovery of the Stuxnet virus in June 2010 was not exactly designed to be "equal," but a strong reaction did occur. It included the development of domestic and international protocols and conventions and several suggestions for the use of new legal principles to ensure the safety of domestic computer systems and tools. For Russia, where ambiguity and suspicion are deeply imbedded in the national tradition, only the worst could be expected from this discovery for Russian national security, and the government reacted accordingly.

The Stuxnet incident struck close to home for three reasons: Russia is home to a plethora of outstanding virus and code writers who quickly understood the advanced nature of the virus and its potential threat to the homeland; the virus's target was a Russian partner in the geopolitical and technical sense; and perhaps most of all, centrifuges

spinning out of control reminded Russia's government and population of their own disasters in the digital and nuclear realm—the 2009
Sayano-Shushenskaya disaster and the 1986 Chernobyl disaster.[2] This
time, while the virus was located outside Russian territory, a new
consequence was under consideration: the virus could potentially
escape Iran and spread to reactors inside Russia. Some analysts suspected that it might already be there.

The virus's use came as a surprise to many Russians. For some, it
signaled the beginning of anonymous cyberattacks on infrastructure.
An added implication was the potential use of such a virus to take out
weapons of mass destruction. Those behind the attacks demonstrated
a rare international boldness (or carelessness, from the Russian perspective) in taking the first major step in the use of a cyberweapon
against infrastructure, a boldness which may not have correctly determined extenuating circumstances and unintended consequences.
The nuclear power reactor the virus was attempting to externally shut
down was at that time (2010) considered an off-limits target. The attack was designed to slow Iran's nuclear enrichment activities, which
had continued unabated after repeated warnings from the international
community to stop attempting to produce weapons-grade material had
had no effect. The Stuxnet attack was designed to be a nonviolent yet
anonymous warning for Iran's failure to take international norms, legal
standards, and the repeated warnings into consideration.

At the plant, as centrifuges spun out of control, monitors showed
all was in working order. The consequences could have been even
worse if a Belarusian scientist had not stumbled across the virus and
warned Russia and other nations of its existence. It is not certain just
how much damage was done to the Iranian reactors. Initial reports
from Russian specialists working at the Bushehr power station stated
that the damage was enormous, but later Iranian reports indicated
that after some initial confusion, everything was back up and running.

THE RUSSIAN RESPONSE

One apparent outcome of the Stuxnet virus was Russia's focus on
quickly upgrading its own computer systems. The nation's rulers did

not want a Stuxnet-type virus to invade Russia's systems and cause havoc or unintended consequences. Stability mattered most, and this required finding a technical way to protect critical infrastructure. Russia's plethora of outstanding code writers immediately went to work to find a defense against Stuxnet's code.

These efforts were matched by the work of the Security Council, Ministry of Foreign Affairs, and Defense Ministry in the development of domestic conventions and international protocols, which are noted below. They were designed to protect Russian computer systems and deter foreign governments from contemplating cyberattacks on Russia. These national and international proposals varied in their goals and objectives. The plans currently proposed, under consideration, or completed include the following:

- "Conceptual Views on the Activities of the Armed Forces of the Russian Federation in Information Space" (2011).[3]
- A "Code of Conduct" letter addressed to the UN General Secretary, along with signatories China, Tajikistan, and Uzbekistan (September 12, 2011).[4]
- A Russian-proposed draft of a United Nations Convention on International Information Security, released at an international meeting of high-ranking officials responsible for security matters in Yekaterinburg, Russia (2011).[5]
- Presidential Decree, "On Creating the State System to Identify, to Prevent, and to Eliminate the Consequences of Cyber Attacks on the Information Resources of the Russian Federation" (January 2013).[6]
- Development of a new cyberspace strategy (2013).[7]
- Development of a cyber command beginning in 2014 (in process).[8]

Some Russian specialists felt the United States did not want any part of the proposed international agreements, since Russia was viewed not only as a source of cyberattacks but also as a potential target of them. At a NATO-Russia Council session in 2011, the Russian

delegation called for an investigation into the Stuxnet incident, indicating their concern over the virus's source.[9]

A look at the definitional aspects of these documents follows.

**"Conceptual Views on the Activities of the Armed Forces of
the Russian Federation in Information Space."** This document
defines terms and offers principles (legality, priority, integration, interaction, cooperation, and innovation) to guide the activities of the
Armed Forces in information space. It elaborates on these principles
as follows: legality means respect for national sovereignty and non-
interference in the internal affairs of other states; priority means the
collection of relevant and reliable information regarding threats and
protection of information resources; integration means the utilization of a coordinated and unified system to enhance the capabilities of the system as a whole; interaction means the coordination of
defense activities with other federal executive bodies; cooperation
means the development of global-level collaboration to detect and
prevent information and technological threats to peace, settle disputes involving these assets, build confidence regarding the use of
trans-boundary information systems, and ensure the secure use of
common information space; and innovation means the recruitment
of skilled personnel. The "Conceptual Views" includes rules for the
use of information space when it is used as an agent of conflict deterrence, prevention, and resolution. It includes confidence-building
measures as well as national concepts for ensuring information space
security and exchanging information promptly about crisis events. It
also declared that Russia's innovation centers must be able to develop
and produce systems capable of carrying out activities in information
space.

**September 12, 2011 "Code of Conduct" letter addressed to
the UN General Secretary.** This letter offers for UN consideration
an international code of conduct for information security. The code
notes that efforts should be directed at providing developing countries with information technology, that operations consistent with the
objective of ensuring Internet stability are required, and that policy

authority for Internet-related public issues is the sovereign right of states. The latter issue is of particular concern to the US State Department, since it implies that citizens of these countries will not have full access to the Internet, but only to those portions deemed essential by the signatory countries.

2011 Convention on International Information Security. The Convention defines terms such as "information war" and "information weapon"; lists principles to follow to safeguard international information security; devotes a section to averting or resolving military conflicts in information space; and lists eleven threats to peace and security in information space. It seeks to regulate the activities of governments to protect international information security and to ensure that the activity of governments in information space will be compatible with an individual's right to seek, receive, and distribute information. However, the Convention further states, "this right may be restricted through legislation to protect the national and social security of each State." Respect must be maintained for the sovereignty of states and their existing political, historical, and cultural specificities. Other chapters in the document are aimed at preventing terrorist use of information space, counteracting illegal activities in information space, and cooperating in the sphere of international information security through confidence-building or consulting activities.

January 15, 2013 Presidential Decree. This decree authorized the Federal Security Service (FSB) to create a state system that could identify, prevent, and eliminate cyberattack consequences on the information resources of the Russian Federation. The FSB was tasked with forecasting situations, providing cooperation among information resource owners, monitoring critical information infrastructure, and determining the causes of cyber incidents in Russia. The FSB must organize this work, develop identification methodologies, define exchange procedures, conduct protection-level measures, develop protection recommendations, and develop home and foreign exchange procedures about cyber incidents.

2013 Cyberspace Strategy. In February 2013, *Kommersant* reported
that the Federation Council was drafting a "Cyberspace Strategy of
the Russian Federation." An analyst for the Center for Policy Studies in Russia noted that this was due to the discovery of Stuxnet
and similar viruses, as well as other factors (social networks, blogs,
and e-banking fraud, among others).[10] It is believed that this strategy was codified in July 2013 as the "Fundamentals of the Russian
Federation's State Policy in the Field of Information Security for the
Period through 2020." Threats to Russia identified in the strategy
include actors using Internet technology as an "information weapon
for military-political, terrorist, and criminal purposes" and for inter-
fering in a state's internal affairs. Russia intends to use the Shanghai
Cooperation Organization, the Collective Security Treaty Organization, and BRICS (the Brazil, Russia, India, China and South Africa
partnership) to help counter these threats. With the assistance of these
organizations, Russia hopes to implement a number of key initiatives,
such as rules of behavior in cyberspace, an internationalized system
for controlling the Internet, and an international legal regime for the
nonproliferation of information weapons.

Cyber command. The Russian Ministry of Defense noted that, in
conjunction with the Prospective Research Foundation, it would be
creating a cyber command in 2014. This new arm of service will operate in both peacetime and wartime environments.[11] There is no official evidence of cyber troops in the Defense Ministry, with only the
Federal Security Service and the Ministry of Internal Affairs possess-
ing such subunits. There were reports in May 2014 that cyber troops
were being trained for the Armed Forces, however, but no other word
on their development has surfaced. One analyst recommended that
there be a center for cyber defense inside the General Staff and at
each military district and fleet. There was also conjecture about the
development of science companies in the Defense Ministry, which
are seen as training bases to produce soldiers for a cyber army.

The new military doctrine of December 26, 2014, specified that
one of the tasks for outfitting the Armed Forces and other troops and

entities with military and special equipment would be the development of information confrontation forces and assets. It is not known if this means the further advancement of such forces, since there has been no authoritative confirmation of their initial development. Upgrading the means of information exchange and creating information control systems integrated with fire control systems and automation equipment are other tasks included in the doctrine.[12]

OTHER RUSSIAN RESPONSES TO STUXNET

Russia, in light of the agreements passed domestically in 2011, looked forward to the October 2012 Budapest Conference on Cybercrime. It hoped that the conference might yield a draft agreement of some sort. This search for an agreement was in response to anxieties in the upper house of Russia's parliament over cyber vulnerabilities. The draft would attempt to fill policy vacuums uncovered by consideration of new cybercrime methods and the Stuxnet incident. The conference reportedly resulted in lengthy discussions regarding the creation of an Internet hotline between the United States and Russia. Russian authorities were also surprised, according to local accounts, at the unexpected advocacy of the acceptance of "standards of responsible conduct of nations" on the Internet by US Secretary of State Hillary Clinton.[13]

At the first forum, which took place in 2013 in London, Russia proposed adopting international rules of conduct on the Internet. Russia presented its concept, "On Information Security," to the UN, which provides Internet regulation standards and seeks to prevent the use of the Internet for military purposes or for toppling regimes.[14] Western countries, however, still consider unlimited freedom of access and self-expression on the Internet more important than sovereignty principles and nonintervention in the internal affairs of other states, which Moscow supports. Western countries also do not agree with the Russian Federation's request to prohibit the development of offensive cyberweapons.

In addition to Russia's domestic and international treaty efforts, individual digital specialists have added their opinions to the mix.

Oleg Demidov, an expert at Russia's Center for Political Studies (PIR-Center), thinks the United States and Russia should agree on prohibiting the use of cyberweapons against financial, nuclear, and industrial assets. The recent use of the Stuxnet virus, he notes, is of particular concern, and the United States risks isolating itself from the international community if it continues using such exotic weapons.[15] Demidov further added that the 2000 Russian Federation Doctrine on Information Security predates Stuxnet, meaning that viruses of this type are not covered in any legal cyber document in Russia.

Of world renown is Eugene Kaspersky, one of the founders of Kaspersky Lab and the producer of an antivirus software sold in the United States. After the Stuxnet attacks, he advocated introducing a digital identity to the Internet to secure access to personal information and banking data. His ideas in 2011 included digital fingerprints, a development added to the Apple 5S phone in 2013.[16] Kasperksy believes the Stuxnet virus will initiate a cyber sabotage exchange in the coming years among nations, now that the cyber genie is out of the bottle.[17]

Another prominent Russian personality who spoke out about Stuxnet was Andrey Krutskikh, who has handled cyber issues for many years for the Russian Foreign Ministry. He often poses a series of legal questions, including whether a cyberattack victim has the right to self-defense and how to determine a proportionate response in case a cyberwar breaks out. Overall, clarity in definitions remains one of his major interests.[18] He was extremely dissatisfied with the so-called *Tallinn Manual* when it appeared, as it was produced by a host of Western specialists who discussed these very questions but left Russians out of the writing and discussion group that produced the document. Upon publication of the manual, a long list of both Defense and Foreign Affairs Ministry specialists in Russia jumped in to criticize the Tallinn group's work.[19]

There was a limited, yet more detailed and interesting response from the Russian military in their journal *Military Thought*. Author A. A. Vorfolomeyev, for example, wrote on the necessity of distinguishing between cyber sabotage, a state-run operation, and cyber terrorism, which usually involves nonstate actors. His analysis included a case study of the Stuxnet virus (using the methodology of fact–fact–conclusion, also known as the principle of induction, according to the author of the article), and noted that this was the first time a virus was created to disrupt an infrastructure site via a large-scale dissemination tool.[20]

Kaspersky Lab estimated that the dissemination of the virus began in March–April 2010. Belarus experts made an initial description of the virus in June 2010. The attack's duration appeared to last for months and took down some 10 percent of the operating centrifuges at the Bushehr facility. Vorfolomeyev argues that Articles 205 (Terrorism) and 281 (Sabotage) of the Russian Criminal Code provide guidance on the legal interpretation of these attacks. He notes that a legal interpretation must first consider objectives and second evaluate the subjective criterion—the goals of the crime. Terrorism usually involves threats or attempts to influence decisionmakers and is limited due to time, available labor resources, and the technical know-how of the terrorists. The latter are limited as well in their ability to collect, process, and analyze information, but they are unlimited in their use of (that is, disregard for) the legal system. Sabotage, on the other hand, involves the disruption of economic or defense activities and is usually associated with state activities. Sabotage involves a much higher authority in terms of international norms granting permission to release a cyber tool than does a terrorist act. The use of information and communication technologies (viruses) may now be considered a more likely point of conflict in the future among states as a result of Stuxnet's release. Such tools may or may not be the result of the activities of a military subunit, as civilian programmers could achieve the same or more likely even better results if the strong collection of code writers who work for businesses around the globe is any indicator.[21]

CONCLUSIONS

On November 12, 2013, the Stuxnet virus once again made the news in Russia. Eugene Kaspersky stated that the virus had hit a Russian nuclear power plant and the international space station, implying that the virus was a "gift that keeps on giving." An external device was the alleged carrier. However, Rosatom (Russian's nuclear agency) stated that they were surprised by Kaspersky's statement, and that all power plants reported no intrusions. The Roscosmos space agency reported the same in regard to the international space station. Kaspersky's claim came at a developer symposium.[22] The purpose for his exposure of this "discovery," which the official agencies denied, is unknown.

To summarize, Russia's reaction to the Stuxnet virus, although slow out of the gate, picked up speed as the realization hit policymakers that agreements, whether domestic or international, were badly needed. Perhaps even more important was the perceived immediate need to lay out legal conditions for nation-states to follow. Causing centrifuges to spin out of control at the Bushehr nuclear power plant must have prompted Russian analysts to mentally rerun the 2009 Sayano-Shushenskaya disaster. A nuclear disaster could only be worse.

Two responses were significant. First, the Russians published three new documents on information security within a year of the discovery of the virus. Second, there appeared to be a desire to draw a legal distinction between nation-state and nonstate involvement in the development of new viruses. The discussion among Russian policymakers quickly updated information based on old paradigms and introduced several new developments that are influencing the current paradigm. The result is a closer look at how Russia's cyber strategy might "cyber cope" in case of future cyber conflict.

Notes

1. Disclaimer: The views expressed in this report are those of the author and do not necessarily represent the official policy or position of the Department of the Army, Department of Defense, or the US government. The Foreign Military Studies Office (FMSO) assesses regional military and security issues through open-source media and direct engagement with foreign military and security specialists to advise army leadership on issues of policy and planning critical to the US Army and the wider military community. Please forward comments referencing this study to:

    FMSO
    ATIN-F MR. THOMAS
    731 MCCLELLAN AVENUE
    FT LEAVENWORTH KANSAS 66027-1350
    COM: (913) 684-5957
    DSN: 552-5957

FAX: (913) 684-5960/5959

E-MAIL: TIMOTHY.L.THOMAS20.CIV@MAIL.MIL

2.   Joe Hasler, writing in *Popular Mechanics* on February 2, 2010, explained the catastrophic accident that took place at the Sayano-Shushenskaya hydroelectric plant. Russia's Federal Service for Ecological, Technological, and Nuclear Supervision (Rostekhnadzor) launched an investigation and blamed poor management and technical flaws for the accident. Repairs on Turbine 2 had been made, and a new automatic control system that slowed or sped up the turbine to match output to fluctuations in power demand was installed. But the system still did not work right, as the amplitude of the machine's vibrations continued to increase to an unsafe level. The unit was taken offline until August 16, when the Bratsk fire forced managers at Sayano-Shushenskaya to push the turbine into service. For more details, see Joe P. Hasler, "Investigating Russia's Biggest Dam Explosion," *Popular Mechanics*, February 2, 2010.

3.   "Conceptual Views on the Activities of the Armed Forces of the Russian Federation in Information Space," Ministry of Defense of the Russian Federation, 2011.

4.   "Letter dated 12 September 2011 from the Permanent Representatives of China, the Russian Federation, Tajikistan, and Uzbekistan to the United Nations addressed to the Secretary-General," Sixty-sixth Session of the United Nations General Assembly, September 14, 2011.

5.   Convention on International Information Security, 2011, http://archive.mid.ru//bdomp/ns-osndoc.nsf/1e5f0de28fe77fdcc32575d900298676/7b17ead7244e2064c3257925003bcbcc!OpenDocument

6.   "President's Decree on Creating the State System to Identify, Prevent, and Eliminate the Consequences of Cyber Attacks on the Information Resources of the Russian Federation," Consultant Plus, January 15, 2013.

7.   Yelena Chernenko, "Peace Be upon Your Domain. Russia Makes Up Its Mind about Information Security Policy," *Kommersant Online*, August 1, 2013, 1, 6.

8.   Aleksandr Stepanov, "Battle of the Computers," Versiya, May 26, 2014.

9.   *Interfax*, January 26, 2011.

10.   "They are proposing to bring to a new level the struggle against cyber crimes. The Federation Council wants to include business and the public in the struggle against cybercrime," *Kommersant*, February 27, 2013, http://www.kommersant.ru/doc-y/2136150.

11.   *Interfax* (in English), October 7, 2013.

12.   Military Doctrine of the Russian Federation, website of the President of Russia, December 26, 2014.

13.   Yelena Chernenko, "Russia and the US to Create Internet Hotlines," *Kommersant Online*, October 9, 2012.

14.   Ibid.

15. "Russia in Search of a Cyber Strategy," *RBC Daily* (Moscow), September 26, 2012, http://www.rbcdaily.ru/politics/562949984792992.

16. "A Future Digital Identity?" *LeFigaro*.fr (Paris), February 21, 2011.

17. Martin Stepanek interview with Eugene Kaspersky, "Powerless Against Cyber Sabotage," *Kurier* (Vienna), March 9, 2011, 13.

18. Comment based on Andrey Krutskikh's presentation at the London Cyber Conference, November 1, 2011.

19. Comments based on Russian Defense and Foreign Ministry presentations in Garmisch, Germany, April 2013.

20. A. A. Vorfolomeyev, "Cyber Sabotage and Cyber Terrorism: Contemporary Limits to the Capabilities of Non-State Actors," *Voyennaya Mysl* (*Military Thought*), No. 12, 2012, 3-11.

21. Ibid.

22. Moscow *Rossiya* 24 TV, November 12, 2013.

"Stuxnet and China"
by J. Stapleton Roy

MEDIA REPORTS THAT THE UNITED STATES and Israel had collaborated to sabotage Iran's nuclear weapons program by introducing the Stuxnet virus into the control system for centrifuges used by Iran for uranium enrichment served to confirm Chinese assumptions that the United States was the leading country in the world seeking to exploit cyber vulnerabilities throughout the globe for intelligence and national security purposes. It reinforced the Chinese view that the United States is hypocritical in portraying China as posing the principal cyber threat to computer systems in the United States and elsewhere.

Stuxnet first burst onto the world scene in July 2010, when media outlets began to report widely the discovery a month earlier of a new type of malicious computer worm. Initially, little was known about the origin and purpose of Stuxnet. Some early reports speculated that the computer worm might have originated in China. Only gradually did it emerge that Stuxnet was targeted at Iran's nuclear facilities and had spread to other countries because of a programing error.

By September 2010, there were Chinese and foreign media reports that Stuxnet was wreaking havoc on computer systems in China. The same month, *Global Times*, the unofficial sister publication of the *People's Daily*, cited reports originating in Iran suggesting that the United States and Israel were behind the malware.[1] In

February 2011, the Chinese newspaper *Liberation Daily* also quoted a *New York Times* report that US and Israeli intelligence organizations had jointly produced the Stuxnet virus.[2] Nevertheless, it took until June 2012, nearly two years from the first widespread reports regarding Stuxnet, for accusations to emerge from Chinese leaders alleging that Stuxnet was a product of a US and Israeli intelligence operation designed to cripple Iran's nuclear weapons program.

Although official Chinese comments on Stuxnet were slow to emerge, unofficial and quasi-official commentators had a field day, using the computer worm to drive home the point that cyberwarfare had entered a new stage, that it posed a serious threat to national "cyber sovereignty," that China was highly vulnerable to such intrusions, and that the United States was hypocritical and two-faced in accusing China of engaging in widespread cyber theft and being the principal threat to global cybersecurity.

Samples of these comments follow, listed in chronological order.[3]

Summary of a *People's Liberation Army Daily* Article by Li Daguang, "After One Opens a 'Pandora's Box' of Cyber Warfare," March 10, 2011[4]

People's Liberation Army Daily invited Li Daguang, the National Defense University professor and cyberwarfare expert who wrote *Information System-based Cyber Operations* [wang luo zuo zhan], to analyze and interpret several recent news events concerning the Internet and cyberwarfare. From the global spread of Stuxnet, which attacked Iran's nuclear facility last November and many suspect was developed by US and Israeli military agencies, it is clear that cyberspace has become a new battlefield involving real fighting at close quarters. History is a reminder that the emergence of any form of warfare is like another "Pandora's box" being opened—the consequence may far exceed human control. Because cyber confrontations have uncontainable and "double-edged sword" effects, their chain effects and threats to global economic security are difficult to predict.

People's Daily (Overseas Edition) Article by Chen Fusheng (Katie Chan), "Spreading Gunpowder Smoke of Cyber Warfare and How We Can Counter It," June 7, 2012[5]

On 28 May, a computer virus dubbed "Flame" was used as a "super cyberweapon" to attack many computers in countries such as Iran. Experts say that this was the most powerful cyberbomb that has been used to date, with a force that is 20 times more destructive than the cyberbomb "Stuxnet" from 2010. At that time, "Stuxnet" damaged the centrifuge used in Iran's nuclear enrichment project.

Facts prove that the first cyberwarfare campaign already started long ago and that this is a problem that is only going to get worse. . . .

Because of the widespread use of computers, all aspects of a country, from the national economy to national defense, and even to people's daily lives, are controlled by the Internet. When the Internet is operating, then the nation is operating, and when the Internet is paralyzed, then the nation is paralyzed. Cyberwarfare is a form of warfare that can cause even more serious harm than traditional land war, naval war, or air war.

Developed countries have the greatest capability for launching cyberwarfare. . . .

The accelerated formulation of a national cyber strategy is an urgently pressing issue. The threat of cyberwarfare must be fully recognized and given full attention. The sense of "cyber sovereignty" must be strengthened. "Cyber sovereignty" is a component of "national sovereignty." We must protect our country's cyber sovereignty against intrusion to ensure the security of the "cyber borders."

Commentary by Xu Peixin, Associate Professor with Communication University of China, "Interpreting the Second Wave of Cyber Security Threats to China," CCTV.com, March 4, 2013[6]

After the failures of the 2003–05 WSIS negotiations, the world was increasingly led by US foreign policy makers and commercial media companies. 2010 onwards has been particularly disastrous. In January 2010, Hillary Clinton delivered a well-known speech at [the] Newseum calling for more Internet freedoms. In March 2010, Google showcased its formal withdrawal from China citing cyberattacks. In May 2010, the Pentagon launched the US Cyber Command, and in May 2010, the US State Department gave 1.5 million dollars to the so-called Global Internet Freedom Consortium directly affiliated with Falun Gong. In June 2010, computer malware Stuxnet—widely believed to be created by [the] US and Israel—was discovered in Iranian and Indonesian computers. In May 2011, President Barack Obama signed an executive order laying out cyberwar guidelines, and two weeks ago, Obama signed a new executive order to strengthen cyber defenses. Most recently, Mandiant released its report titled "APT1: Exposing One of China's Cyber Espionage Units."

Motivated by US attempts to weaponize [the] Internet, nations such as the UK, South Korea, Germany and Iran followed suit to increase cyberwar capabilities. The more energy the United States wastes on accusing and attacking others, the more the world community feels threatened by the US monopoly on Internet governance. The more other nations challenge the United States in forums such as ITU, the more US state authorities and businesses find it necessary to create a scapegoat. US concerns ranging from creating jobs in the Pentagon to bringing jobs home through trade wars will only hurt global economic growth. It is not the way the world works. It is much ado about nothing.

People's Daily Article by Zhong Sheng,"Do Not Treat Cyberspace as a War Theater; Avoid Harming Others and Damaging Oneself," February 27, 2013[7]

In fact, it is the United States that is a hacking empire worthy of the title. According to American media, the United States set up the world's first cyber hacking unit back in 2002. In 2011 the US military formally established [a] Cyber Command. Iran's infrastructure such as its uranium enrichment facility ha[s] been attacked by high-grade viruses such as "Stuxnet," and the black hands behind this are an open secret. US military and intelligence organs attend an annual hackers congress in lofty tone, when top hackers from all over the world gather [at] the Pentagon. American media have all along discussed this with enthusiasm. A recent article in the *Economist* said that the United States is not a new hand in cyber espionage. Officials of France's cyber monitoring departments claim that during the French presidential election last year the United States used espionage software to get into then–President Sarkozy's computer. In 2012 attacks originating from the United States easily headed the list of external cyberattacks on China.

People's Daily Article by Zhong Sheng, "Blackening China Can Hardly Conceal the Evil Behavior of the 'Hackers' Empire,'" May 8, 2013[8]

As everyone knows, the United States is the true "hackers' empire," and its extensive cyber espionage activities are not only aimed at hostile countries but also at allies; its intelligence gathering scope includes the political, military, science and technology, and commercial fields. In recent years the United States has continually strengthened its cyber tools for political subversion of other countries. Ever since the Internet was born, the United States has prepared to fight a cyber war, and has created many world firsts.

. . .The United States was the first country to carry out virtual cyberwar. According to reports, the history of US cyberwar can be traced back to the first Gulf War. In 2011, American media revealed a cyberwar plan codenamed "Olympic Games." When Iran's uranium enrichment centrifuges were attacked by the "Stuxnet" virus, the sinister hands behind this have long been an open secret.

. . . While vigorously hyping up the "theory of China's cyber threat," US steps in expanding its cyber forces and preparing for war are forging ahead at great speed. Despite the big cut in military expenditure[s], the United States plans a five-fold expansion of the Cyber Command establishment, and its spending on cybersecurity will show a big rise to $17.7 billion in 2014. NATO put forward the "Tallinn Manual on International Law Applicable to Cyber Warfare" in March 2013. Although this is not an official NATO manual, its viewpoint is precisely the same as the US State Department view, and obviously wants to put a cloak of legality on US cyberwarfare.

As the above examples illustrate, Chinese commentators have not been hesitant to read far-reaching implications into the use of Stuxnet for cyberwarfare attacks. Wu Zhenglong, the author of the February 10, 2011 *Liberation Daily* commentary "Stuxnet's Warning" summarized above, concluded that "Without doubt, 'Stuxnet' not only opened a new era in the military cyber defense revolution, but also permanently changed international Internet security. Cyberattacks will become one of the most severe non-traditional security issues faced by mankind in the new period. In order to preserve minimum order in the life and work of mankind, international society has the duty and responsibility to act to formulate the necessary international laws and treaties, rigorously prevent misuse of cyber viruses, and rigorously prevent cyberattacks on civil facilities so that an orderly and controllable international cybersecurity regime can be ensured."[9] Chinese commentators also used the example of Stuxnet to underscore the need for China to tighten its own Internet security procedures. A commentary on China Youth On Line (cyol.net), the website of the China Youth Daily, dated March 1, 2013, referred to Stuxnet and then discussed the threat posed by Cisco and other foreign equipment companies whose products to varying degrees contained technical security gaps, noting that Cisco's VoIP telephone service had a flaw that permitted hackers to implant malicious code and steal the content of telephone conversations. The commentary also noted that the data centers of China's four largest banks and of commercial banks in cities throughout China all used Cisco equipment and that Cisco had over 70 percent of the market for Chinese financial companies.[10]

Another commentary on *Xinhuawang* on August 19, 2013, noted that because of security concerns, China would be investigating IBM, Oracle, and EMC. Citing the example of the Stuxnet attack on Iran's nuclear research program, the commentary stated that both before and after Stuxnet there had been other viruses, all of which had utilized the Microsoft Windows operating system.[11]

Especially in the early months after the discovery and spread of the Stuxnet virus, some Chinese reports took on an alarmist quality. In a lengthy discussion of the Stuxnet virus on November 12, 2010, by Hexun Technology, the thrust of the commentary was that Stuxnet posed a major threat to China's manufacturing industry, which the authors speculated may have been a secondary target of the virus. The commentary noted that Siemens was one of the largest foreign suppliers of computers for Chinese industry and that Siemens-developed systems were widely used in many of China's most important sectors, such as energy, electric power, communications, and transportation. It cited a *Reference News* report from the Xinhua News Agency stating, "In recent days the virus has infected six million computers, affecting nearly one thousand factories and industrial facilities, and the original servers for the attack on China possibly came from the United States."[12]

Based on the material reviewed for this report, one can draw a number of conclusions from the Chinese reaction to the information that progressively emerged regarding the Stuxnet attack on the Iranian centrifuge control systems:

1. The Chinese were impressed by the sophistication of the attack.
2. They quickly recognized the vulnerability of their own systems and infrastructure to damage or shutdown from cyberattacks using Stuxnet-like viruses and worms.

3. The attribution of Stuxnet to the United States and Israel confirmed their suspicions that the United States was devoting major resources to developing cyberwarfare capabilities.

4. The evidence suggesting that the United States, along with Israel, was the first country to mount a cyberattack on the basic infrastructure of another country confirmed their assumption that the United States was aggressively exploiting the Internet and cyberspace for intelligence collection and the advancement of national security interests.

5. The information regarding Stuxnet reinforced pre-existing Chinese caution regarding overdependence on foreign information systems technology.

6. The Chinese quickly recognized the propaganda potential for exploiting the revelations regarding Stuxnet, later supplemented by the Edward Snowden material, to counter US accusations that China was the leading perpetrator of cyber theft.

7. Because of China's own vulnerabilities, one element in the Chinese reaction to Stuxnet was the strengthening of their willingness to explore with the United States and other countries the formulation of international ground rules regarding the exploitation of cyberspace for malicious attacks on other countries.

8. Chinese commentary did not dwell on the positive aspect of the Stuxnet attack in slowing Iran's nuclear weapons program.

As a final word, one can say that Stuxnet did not disillusion the Chinese regarding US behavior in cyberspace, since they had long recognized the US lead in information technology and were actively exploiting cyberspace themselves for intelligence and information gathering purposes.

Notes

1. *Global Times*, September 27, 2010.

2. Wu Zhenglong, "Stuxnet's Warning," *Jiefang Ribao*, February 10, 2011.

3. These samples of material translated by the Open Source Center (OSC) were provided by Audrye Wong of the Carnegie Endowment for International Peace.

4. Li Daguang, "After One Opens a 'Pandora's Box' of Cyber Warfare," *People's Liberation Army Daily*, March 10, 2011, translated by OSC, CPP20110622088001.

5. Katie Chan (Chen Fusheng), "Spreading Gunpowder Smoke of Cyber Warfare and How We Can Counter It (Watchtower)," *People's Daily* (Overseas Edition), June 7, 2012, translated by OSC, CPP20120607787001.

6. Commentary by Xu Peixin, "Interpreting the Second Wave of Cyber Security Threats to China," CCTV.com, March 4, 2013, also provided by Audrye Wong, Carnegie Endowment for International Peace.

7. Zhong Sheng, "Do Not Treat Cyberspace as a War Theater; Avoid Harming Others and Damaging Oneself," *People's Daily*, February 27, 2013, translated by OSC, CPP20130227702002.

8. Zhong Sheng, "Blackening China Can Hardly Conceal the Evil Behavior of the 'Hackers' Empire,'" *People's Daily*, May 8, 2013, translated by OSC, CPP20130508787003.

9. Wu Zhenglong, "Stuxnet's Warning," *Jiefang Ribao*, February 10, 2011, translation by the author.

10. China Youth On Line (cyol.net), China Youth Daily, March 1, 2013, http://zqb.cyol.com/html/2013-03/01/nbs.D110000zgqnb_01.htm.

11. *Xinhuawang*, August 19, 2013, http://finance.huanqiu.com/data/2013-08/4261364.html.

12. Hexun Technology, November 12, 2010, http://www.360doc.com/content/10/1207/23/443827_75990773.shtml.

"Iran's Reaction to Stuxnet" by Nader Uskowi

THE 2009-10 CYBERATTACKS ON IRAN'S uranium enrichment unit at Natanz destroyed nearly a thousand centrifuges. Stuxnet targeted the Siemens SCADA system at Natanz, making it the first known malware capable of spreading by itself, hiding itself, and attacking by itself. By targeting industrial systems to gain particular strategic and political advantages, Stuxnet showed the path to the future of cyberwar.

In June 2012, the *New York Times* reported that Stuxnet was part of a joint US and Israeli intelligence operation to slow down Iran's nuclear program. The Iranian officials regard cyberattacks against the country as part of a larger US campaign to destroy Iran's infrastructure and its economy, paving the way for an eventual regime change in Tehran.

Iran initially was unable to mitigate the spread of Stuxnet, but since has developed comprehensive plans and devoted substantial resources to computer network defense and retaliatory offensive cyberattacks targeting the United States and its allies. Still in its initial stages, the Iranian cyber program has the potential to make the country a serious player in global cyber conflict.

INITIAL REACTION

It is believed that the Iranian authorities were in total darkness as to what had caused the spinning problems of the centrifuges at Natanz and their destruction. Iran lost some one thousand IR-1 centrifuges at the enrichment unit out of nine thousand units then in operation. There are indications now that the morale among Natanz managers and engineers had become seriously low.

Following the public discovery of the infection in mid-2010, the Iranians, unable to stop the spread of Stuxnet, invited foreign experts to fight the infection.

The regime, however, mobilized its resources soon to fight what it perceived as the start of a US campaign to destroy its nuclear program without firing a shot. This author understands that Iran's Supreme Leader Ayatollah Ali Khamenei gathered senior security officials, warning that the attack on Natanz was part of a larger plot, along with sanctions, to destroy Iran's infrastructure and its economy.

Khamenei to this day, despite recent overtures by Iran's new president toward improving bilateral relations with the United States and notwithstanding President Obama's recent declaration at the United Nations, believes that the US strategy is still regime change in Iran and partition of the country. Khamenei believes Iran's nuclear program is but an excuse to attack Iran. He considers the presence of US forces in the Persian Gulf as proof of this strategy and as a threat to Iranian national security. It is through such a viewpoint that Khamenei and his senior advisors regard the Stuxnet attack as a manifestation of the overall US strategy in Iran.

DEFENSIVE MEASURES

Stuxnet made the Iranian leadership at its highest levels aware of the importance of critical network security as it exposed the country's inability to remove the worm from its systems. Since then, Iran has significantly increased resources devoted to computer network defense and has refocused its cyber defense posture. It has elevated the role and responsibilities of its national cybersecurity authority, involved its major research universities in cybersecurity, and strengthened the cyber departments within the Ministry of Information and Security and the Iranian Revolutionary Guard Corps' Quds Force (QF).

The subsequent discovery in 2012 of "Flame," a massive spy malware program that had infiltrated Iranian computers, reinforced Iranian cyber defense priorities. Flame is believed to have targeted Iran's oil ministry and its main export terminal at Kharq Island. Russia's antivirus firm Kaspersky Lab said at the time of the virus's discovery that Flame might have been operating in the wild as early as 2007. Whereas Stuxnet was designed to damage Natanz centrifuges, Flame, while sharing characteristics with Stuxnet, was built to spy on the country's computer networks and send back intelligence. The United States and Israel were also suspected of creating Flame.

In mid-October 2012, Iran's newly completed Bushehr nuclear power reactor experienced a near-explosion. The authorities shut it down temporarily and removed fuel rods from the plant. Later, Iran said that Stuxnet was back and had tampered with the reactor's computers.

The Iranians later talked about a massive conspiracy involving major antivirus firms to keep the existence of Stuxnet and Flame hidden for an extended period of time. That theory notwithstanding, Stuxnet went undetected for more than a year after it was launched in the wild, even though a zero-day exploit that was used in the virus had reportedly been used before with another piece of malware, Duqu, which had also infiltrated Iranian computers. Iranian technicians soon realized that Stuxnet, Duqu, and Flame were not easily detectable malware. They were probably created by Western intelligence agencies as part of an ongoing cyberwarfare campaign.

In the aftermath, the National Cyber Security Committee (NCSC) has become an important organ in Iran's national security apparatus. The MAHER Computer Emergency Response Team (CERT) Coordination Center was formed by the Ministry of Information and Communications Technology to oversee critical network security. On the military side, Iran's Passive Defense Organization is heavily involved in cyber preparedness. In October 2012, it held the first-ever cyber drill in six major zones in the country to test cyber infrastructure.

Iran is also developing a nationally dedicated Internet, the Iran National Data Network. Although its creation might have more to do with the desire on the part of the authorities to control the flow of information between the country's citizens and the outside world, the so-called "clean Internet" is billed as a first line of defense against foreign cyberattacks.

Iran has also been trying to develop indigenous antivirus firms to block the use of foreign-built software. If Iran's missile program is any indication, the Iranians could also attempt to reverse-engineer Stuxnet for launching their own attacks against industrial systems in the West.

OFFENSIVE/RETALIATORY MEASURES

Soon after the Stuxnet discovery, Iran began retaliatory cyberattacks against US, Saudi, and Israeli targets. Its computer network operations were also meant to project an image of national strength in cyber conflicts. The Distributed Denial of Service (DDoS) attacks against some twenty major US banks began in September 2011, and are likely to continue. The Iranians focused their attacks on the data centers used to host services in the "cloud" to commandeer massive computing power to back substantial DDoS attacks against bank websites. The use of data centers against so many US financial institutions was indeed the first major achievement of Iranian cyber actors. They elevated DDoS attacks to a new high, manifested in the unprecedented scale, scope, and effectiveness of their attacks.

In June 2012, the Iranians breached Saudi Aramco's network. It is believed Iran will continue targeting rival oil companies in the Persian Gulf as a top computer network operations priority. Iranian actors are also believed to have targeted the US Navy/Marine Corps Intranet.

THE QUDS FORCE AND MINISTRY OF INTELLIGENCE AND SECURITY

The IRGC's Quds Force (QF) has established an active and growing department for electronic warfare, and has become Iran's key offensive cyberwarfare actor, also directing the cyberattack operations of a number of local hacking contractors. The QF is organized to direct asymmetrical war on behalf of Iran in the region and beyond in case of a military conflict with the West. And cyberwarfare is increasingly becoming an important element in the QF's mission. The tight relationships between the QF and militant organizations in the region, like the Lebanese Hezbollah, Shia militias in Syria and Iraq, and other affiliates in Afghanistan and the Persian Gulf, will give the organization the resources necessary to establish a region-wide cyber threat network. Inside Iran, the Ministry of Intelligence and Security and its growing network of local hacking contractors are the country's active cyber actors.

IRAN AND CYBERWARS

Iranian cyber actors have quickly gained the ability and experience to target financial and energy sectors and are attempting to exploit vulnerabilities in the Western defense sector as well.

As shown during the DDoS attacks on US banks, they can indeed cause significant short-term disruptions in their targets.

The state has provided unprecedented resources to safeguard its network security and to launch retaliatory attacks against the United States and its allies. The Quds Force in particular has become a major cyber actor with the resources to establish a regional cyber network threating the countries in the Persian Gulf and beyond.

The question is how quickly the Iranians could gain the expertise to launch complex computer network attacks. Their DDoS attacks on US banks show their willingness and desire to experiment with new ways of launching cyberattacks. Their attempts to reverse-engineer sophisticated viruses cannot be discounted.

The World after Stuxnet

"Confidence-Building Measures after Stuxnet: Opportunities and Incentives" by Robert Fonow

W<small>E HAVE ARRIVED AT A</small> paradigm shift in international relations, in the sense that Thomas Kuhn identified it: a series of developments and events leading to a recognition that formerly useful ways of understanding the world around us have changed. The shift to the Internet as a weapons platform has been developing for a long time. But only within the last fifteen years have telecommunications and the Internet become understood as areas of significant interest for governments, rising from low politics to a standard item on the international negotiating agenda, although it seems that intelligence services are well ahead of politicians.

Paradigm shifts are the result of innovation, and usually technological innovation rather than, for example, a new or different political philosophy. Marxism's rise and decline was not a paradigm shift, though it has been described as such by those who credited it with scientific predictability. One could even argue that the advent of fission weapons was not a paradigm shift, although it happened with unprecedented speed and urgency. Both Marxism and nuclear weapons remained bounded by a known and understood political system:

the system of states. Marxism was contained within the system. Nuclear weapons were immediately recognized as so destructive that everyone understood the need for strict state and government control. The Internet is unbounded by the same rules.

I prefer to see the Internet in historical terms, as a development, or even an application layer, on the international telecommunications network that has been developing for 150 years. Treating cyberwarfare as a dimension of the international telecommunications system rather than a mysterious development of the Internet provides a greater array of responses to the issues of post-Stuxnet cybersecurity, and greater possibilities for confidence-building measures.

Since the beginning of international telecommunications, there has been a fuzzy demarcation between military and commercial network use. In the mid-1980s, the military impact of network technology was so obvious it became known as the Revolution on Military Affairs in the United States and popularized in organizations like the International Institute for Strategic Studies in London. Networks provided the technical foundation for two wars in Iraq.

Some in the British school of international affairs, with which I identify, primarily based in the London School of Economics (LSE)'s department of international relations, argued that the early Internet was another in a long line of functional technologies—referring to David Mitrany's functionalism and neo-functionalism—that led to a beneficial result for humanity, and was then perverted to military and destructive uses.[1] That would make data communications technologies indistinguishable in a long line of neutral technologies.

I happen to think that functionalism has a lot to say about the positive, normative influence of technology in international affairs. Mitrany argues that greater interdependence in the form of technical and social ties between countries can lead to peaceful relations, using the post-war development of the European Community as an example, and that most cooperation between states is developed by technical or "functional" experts in fields like posts and telecommunications, medicine, and even finance—not by politicians. Yes and no. History also shows that those who maintain a technological lead in defense are precisely those societies with the freedom and internal institutional strength to develop theories like functionalism. International cooperation depends on a political desire for functional expressions of cooperation to develop. So when a paradigm shift as radical as offensive cyberwarfare occurs, it is wise to stay in front of technological developments. That is a given, but it is also wise to set boundaries on its application and uses, or at least understand where potential boundaries might be drawn.

And here we are today: discussing Stuxnet and the offensive use of cyber technologies, trying to understand where they can and cannot be used with some level of efficiency and effectiveness, and—like the ladders of escalation in limited nuclear war forty years ago—looking for ways to manage perilous circumstances.

A TURNAROUND MANAGER'S VIEW

I am in the latter stages of a career in international telecommunications, begun with the US Air Force and National Security Agency at the age of eighteen. My career has included corporate, government, and consulting work in many countries. My particular technical expertise in international telecommunications is the development of the infrastructure for data communications from telex to early packet switching through Internet technologies.

Those who have read my writing for the Center for Technology and National Security Policy (CTNSP) at the National Defense University and within the Department of Defense (DoD) know that I remain more concerned about the damage that kinetic attacks can do to the global system than I am about cyber activities. To me, cybersecurity and cyberwarfare are applications that ride the infrastructure. Almost any cyberattack can be contained as long as the infrastructure remains intact. A systematic attack on the infrastructure renders cyber anything useless.

Within the international telecommunications business, I am also a turnaround manager, usually dealing with distressed operations—those where management has made bad decisions, where a technology opportunity was missed, or even where a government has misstepped—there are many reasons why organizations get into trouble. In this role, I have been deeply involved in the reconstruction of Iraq's telecom and IT systems over several years, which is widely acknowledged as a success. I also reside in Beijing, and so I have an abiding interest in containing any problems between the United States and China.

Confidence-building measures are a matter of course in any turn-around, always necessary in distressed operations, recovery from crises, or in a significant transformation. So allow me to approach the issue of confidence-building measures in cyberwarfare as a China-based American turnaround manager with a predilection for peaceful resolution of international problems.

As a turnaround manager, I use a dialectical approach to problem solving—thesis, antithesis, and synthesis: assess the situation, look for options, test options, decide what I can and cannot give away in a negotiation, apply what works, and discard what does not. It is the same approach I have used in two turnarounds in China, and also in Iraq. My work is operational. I am hired to get things done. I usually work under some type of predefined goal or a strategic framework. Turnaround managers are focused on goals and, while we can be diplomatic, turnaround managers and reconstruction officials are not diplomats. But, like good diplomats, we value confidence-building measures as building blocks to success. CBMs require the navigation of a political and strategic landscape.

I am not certain yet to what degree this dialectic will work in containing the possibility of post-Stuxnet cyberwarfare. It is most likely to work in functional, technical sectors, underneath a strategic framework.

THE CURRENT OPERATIONS ENVIRONMENT

According to many global commentators, the United States has un-leashed the world's first cyberwarfare offensive weapon, or at least the first software acknowledged to be a weapon. Some of the comments seem to have at least quasi-official US backing and serve three purposes: first, to assure the world that Stuxnet has a shelf life of danger for most users; second, to warn that bad actors with skills could take the product and develop it, so it is best for other governments to keep a wary eye out and work with the United States to contain any outbreaks; and third, to let the world (and particularly China) know that the United States is far ahead of any competitor in cyberwarfare activities—so be very careful in what you are hacking into in the United States.

There is much concern about hacking today, particularly surrounding attacks from China. Press reports in China, however, indicate an acknowledgement that cyber development lags far behind the United States. For example, almost all observers say that the United States dwarfs China in cybersecurity funding. The consensus seems to be that the United States spends around $6.5 billion and China $400 million annually on cybersecurity. The United States holds the advantage.

All hacking is opportunistic. If cyber defenses are weak, then Chinese, US, Russian, Serbian, Nigerian, and other hackers will attack them. Many of the opportunities for hacking come from the peculiarities of an unregulated or lightly-regulated economic system, especially one characterized by a mergers and acquisitions system that excites Wall Street and Washington politicians but creates the kludges and reduced IT budgets for CIOs that leave so many back doors open.

In my limited talks so far with Chinese telecom academics, infrastructure protection remains the main topic of conversation. Faculties are not ready to teach cybersecurity. The best Chinese position to defend against a cyberattack from the United States would be to isolate the infrastructure—for example, to cut cables or turn off the electronics in international gateways if a threat is underway or perceived to be imminent.

National networks can be isolated. There are no predefined protocols for what a nation will accept in remaining connected to the global network in response to an attack. Several countries believe that multilateral venues are the place to develop these protocols. I presume this is behind the thinking of Russia and China at the International Telecommunication Union recently. They do not want their networks under US control. The system worked well under the ITU for more than a hundred years before the Internet. To me, this is an understandable position.

As a consequence of recent revelations of the scale and depth of US cyber capabilities, the Chinese central government has advised banks and strategic industries to remove US and international equipment and invest in Chinese-produced networking equipment. To what degree the Chinese economy can withstand this, or an attack, is unknown. It is possible that the banking industry could revert to legacy communications in the short- and medium-term, depending on how much is left in exchanges and warehouses.[2] X.75, X.25, and even HF remain reliable systems, if obsolete, which could support core governance and economic transactions. China can cut off web access and common cellphone services in a crisis to maintain enough capacity for continued government communications. This would be a temporary measure while Huawei and ZTE ramp up production of advanced systems and storage.

To say that all nations spy on militaries but only China engages in commercial cyber espionage sounds whiny and silly in Beijing. However, not responding to this activity shows weakness and undermines international conventions. Telecom executives might argue that the world cannot continue to let Chinese officials and businesspeople ignore agreements and conventions without corrupting the entire international system.

Where does continued Chinese hacking of economic targets elicit a technical response? IP theft is not a divine right of the ancient Middle Kingdom, or excusable on the basis of a historical humiliation, or a victim playing catch-up, or simple expediency, or whatever it is. The United States cannot make decisions based on intentions—only on actions and their results. What we do know is that China is an economically expansionist state at a time when the United States is under a number of stresses, most of its own making, that limit its responses. There are also a significant number of elite policymakers, academics, and businesspeople in China who consider the United States to be bought and paid for thanks to Beijing's holdings of US Treasury bills; in other words, under control.

The political threat is that a revisionist consensus develops in Washington arguing that focusing on the Middle East and Islamic jihad was a grave mistake that let China undermine US economic and intellectual capital. Undertones of this exist in Washington already— China's inflicting of a death by a thousand cuts on the US economy. We are then forced into a coercive diplomacy where cyberwar becomes considered a valid option. Better to develop CBMs now.

FIRST STEPS

In such a hostile and suspicious environment, straightforward approaches to confidence-building measures are unlikely to be successful. CBMs will have to be realistic and backed up with teeth. James McGregor, a Beijing-based author and commentator, notes that the current US position is so weak that diplomats are left to convince Beijing that their ideas for cooperating and adhering to agreements are in China's interest.[3] A more promising approach would be a negotiating strategy based on negative, positive, and neutral incentives. Confidence-building measures are social work.

NEGATIVE INCENTIVES

Negative incentives always require a firmness of purpose. The power of Wall Street, retailers, and the American Chamber of Commerce in China (Amcham China) to interfere in attempts to influence China's negative activities should not be underestimated. Those who do well in any endeavor are interested in maintaining the status quo. It is a global economy, with many players identifying themselves as global citizens.

For two years, I was a co-chair of Amcham China's ICT Forum, advocating for a tougher approach to negotiations on market access. I was consistently shut down by some of the companies that China now wants to kick out. This extended to even holding a seminar on the subject of market access, which was tabled in fear that it would annoy the Ministry of Industry and Information Technology. The companies that are established do not want trouble, and they do not want competition, as they have enjoyed a quasi-monopoly in China in exchange for their cooperation on technology transfer, at least until now.

What are possible negative options?

Option 1: The Chinese government has ordered strategic industries to remove equipment and software from the "eight dragons" (Microsoft, Qualcomm, Intel, Google, Oracle, IBM, Cisco, and Apple) as a response to surveillance and the Snowden revelations. The Chinese appear to be surprised by the scale of surveillance—though surely this is posturing. Anyone with an understanding of intelligence, increases in network speed, and the lower and lower cost of storage should assume that what can be stored will be stored, and China is no exception. The difference is that Snowden's revelations have removed the veil of propriety and exposed hypocrisy in both countries. As a consequence, what might have been left unfunded in China is now being funded. What domestic purchases might have been left to a date when Chinese technology is closer in capability to its US counterparts are now being purchased on accelerated time frames.

Stopping major international equipment suppliers from prospering in China is not an empty threat, but one that merits careful consideration. Starting in the mid-1990s, Sprint built significant parts of the Chinese Internet using Cisco equipment. Today, each of these dragon companies is deeply integrated into the Chinese economy.

The US response so far points to a cross-generational change in the status of the China-US relationship. Older executives and government officials are concerned that banning US equipment might damage the relationship, and are ready to enter into negotiations with Chinese authorities to maintain market access. However, younger US managers seem to be ready for a confrontation.

Many younger technologists believe that the current generation of Chinese leaders has let US technical and business leadership slip away due to corporate greed and intellectual property theft. These technologists have a more realistic sense of competitive international relations, not one necessarily based on globalization at any cost. They are quite content to let the Chinese government and state-owned enterprises rely on Huawei and ZTE equipment exclusively, and in their minds, pick up the pieces later on in a more cooperative environment.

Foreign technical trade associations in China are considered by their members and supporters to be doing their best, and should try to maintain a dialogue with the government in Beijing, but there is no expectation that China will enter into serious negotiations over technology policy. More and more companies are reassessing decisions about what will be exported and what will not. International lawyers tell me, anecdotally, that much of their business is wrapping up ventures. Google set an early precedent others may have wished they could or thought they should follow.

In China, older officials are convinced that the Communist Party has surpassed the United States in political and organizational efficiency. But it is likely that most government officials, especially at the highest, most-isolated level, have little understanding of the nation's domestic and international dependence on networking technology and applications. Younger officials are more knowledgeable and realistic.

Concern about Snowden's NSA revelations may have kickstarted a renewed interest in cybersecurity, but any change will take a lot of time to filter down through the Chinese policy system, making it unlikely that China will significantly improve its security technologies in the short- and mid-term future, which gives the advantage to the United States. This seems to be the consensus among the technically knowledgeable in the United States with its large multinational population, including many Indians in high places, and also in Germany. Let the Chinese use their own equipment. Maybe it works, maybe not. There is a lot more to putting a national network together than kit.

Younger generations of both Chinese and US technologists are aware of the disparity, and this is where the possibility for negotiations exists. Take this option off the diplomacy table. Do not overreact.

Option 2: The United States is the graduate school of China. China's twelfth Five-Year Plan for strategic emerging industries will not reach even modest success without access to the technical research and PhD programs of US universities. Innovation depends on diverse inputs. This is the history of San José, Seattle, Boston, and New York City, where research programs and companies include many national cultural inputs in design, software engineering, and development. Chinese Internet and networking technologies and services remain almost completely derivative, and dependent upon a protected—though large—domestic network that minimizes the opportunity for foreign participation.

Visa restrictions do not have to be omnibus, but selective visa restrictions are a point of leverage where there seem to be few.

Option 3: Strict access to investment in US technical companies. China lacks an infrastructure for innovation. The largest Internet monopolies, with huge resources gained as favored companies in the Chinese political system, are attempting to invest heavily in US technical companies. Controlled access to funding mechanisms are also a negative incentive.

POSITIVE INCENTIVES

The telecom and IT sector provide several opportunities that might offer a path toward nonconfrontational growth and collaboration or cooperation.

Option 4: There is little downside to the United States taking a cooperative position on international management of the Internet and international telecommunications system. This means resuming a cooperative leadership position within the International Telecommunication Union, which became a specialized agency of the UN in 1949. The ITU has contributed immensely to peaceful international relations for more than 150 years, making it the most successful diplomatic organization in history. To work against it is to work against history.

The United States may own the Internet routing methods and addressing schemes that are the World Wide Web, but it does not have any particular ownership of the cables, switching centers, or specialized SCADA and satellite networks that also use the international telecommunications network. Some humility is recommended.

The Internet freedom agenda is terminally damaged. There is little to lose in giving up some control of the Internet's management system. There is no inherent danger in a world of bilateral and multilateral interconnection agreements. The United States will have the support of fee-seeking lawyers around the world. US intelligence services are comprehensive and multifaceted. Clever and resourceful, they will find workarounds.

The confidence-building measure here is in playing China and Russia at their own game. If the United States accepts, China and Russia lose the high road. The ITU is where global protocols for containing cyber conflict can be negotiated. The United States can negotiate toward its interests, winning some points and giving some away in a cooperative spirit. There are advantages for US corporations and companies when the US government is seen as constructive rather than obstructive.

Option 5: Concentrate on a tangential technical issue: physical security. No one has an interest in seeing the Internet infrastructure damaged. A kinetic attack on a surprisingly small number of facilities in strategic locations could cause very serious damage to the international economic and banking system. Agreeing on a restoration protocol in which China would play an important role with its manufacturing capacity seems like a good place to start.

NEUTRAL INCENTIVES (GENERAL GLOBAL CONCERNS)

Option 6: International Internet crime (deep Internet). Internet crime is an emerging field with several international dimensions. The Chinese government has a serious international corruption problem. Vast sums are leaving the country via illicit or legally-undefined ways. The new Chinese government is publicly committed to anti-corruption policies. The US Treasury Department, meanwhile, has an elaborate program to find and return hidden cash and other deposits. Treasury and US intelligence will have a good idea where the money is located, or at least will have search regimes and relationships that could be shared.

Option 7: Other infrastructure issues (electrical grid). Many people suggest that securing each country's electrical grid is a priority for confidence-building measures. The problem with the electrical grid is its status as a valid military target. You could not have military planning without some consideration of attacking power supplies.

It is possible that protocols regarding infrastructure attacks can be established, but they are likely to be narrow. Any areas with direct military applications will make general confidence-building measures difficult to achieve.

Militaries may be able to develop confidence-building measures confined to military escalation. China has elaborate CBMs with India to quickly resolve border disputes, but these were developed after a period of conflict when both sides were able to assess the advantages and disadvantages of CBMs.

IMPROVING THE CBM ENVIRONMENT

CONTROL THE NSA—WHO IS IN CHARGE?

An American living or working abroad and reading international newspapers would get the impression that the head of the NSA is a peer competitor to the president of the United States. They appear to trade policy options over which the president has limited control. Any confidence-building measures would need our interlocutors to trust the integrity of the US political system, or at least understand its potential for adversarial loyalty.

It appears also that the US government is near a state of war with its largest companies in the cyber domain. The government does not necessarily see them as enemies, but does see them at least as intellectual adversaries. Google and Yahoo! try to protect global data streams, while the NSA considers intercepting and analyzing them an intellectual challenge. The whole affair is redolent of a network-based computer game, without sufficient thought to the implications and outcomes.

We can do it, so we should do it: foster increases in processing power, exponential bandwidth growth, and unlimited storage capacity. The advantage goes to the most sophisticated gamers, which depends on where they were trained, their exposure to other gamers, ease of network access, and English capability: all things that give the United States an advantage.

The NSA is a technologically agnostic organization of engineers, and as engineers, its members are not consumed with political ideology. They go with what works, with whatever they can get their hands on and their minds around. Today's activities are simply an extension of this mindset. Intel, EMC, and lightwave technologies that provide exponential increases in fiber-optic cable bandwidth simply give them bigger tools. There is nothing else that I can see that would make the organization less susceptible to political control, and their activities even a bargaining chip in a negotiation.

UNDERSTAND THE ACTORS

A unilateral US government position on post-Stuxnet negotiations based on the current Internet freedom agenda is unlikely to achieve results. The White House and State Department can provide a desired outcome, but are unlikely to be the key facilitators at the moment. The international telecommunications system, where Stuxnet and cyberwar resides, is returning to a multilateral form of decisionmaking. If confidence-building measures are desired, multilateral fora are the most likely place to get commitments on their acceptance.

Most global corporations are also constrained as profit-making enterprises responsible to shareholders with short-term interests. They will have limited resources for serious long-term negotiations. US corporations can suggest confidence-building measures on the Mitrany model, since there is a separation between companies and government in the United States. The same conditions do not exist in China, where the Communist Party and corporations are for most purposes the same organization. Government controls business without demarcation. Party officials are the business leaders. Winners are chosen; they do not emerge. But there are at least some common interests between Western corporations and Chinese state-owned mega industries.

Foundations and academia seem to be the most promising vehicles for confidence-building, since they have no executive authority and can define confidence-building measures in a nonconfrontational environment. However, once defined, these must transfer to governments and service providers.

CONCLUSION

The best approach to confidence-building measures post-Stuxnet is to strengthen the multilateral defenses inherent in the system of states. This means negotiating multilateral telecommunications and Internet agreements and confidence-building measures in good faith, particularly at the ITU.

In this new environment, in which cyberweapons can cause serious damage and disruption, a realistic approach to policy and negotiations is required. There is no need to consider multilateral negotiations as weak or erring on the side of niceness. Any US policy must go with what works, which is likely to result in a stronger and more cooperative approach to multilateral agreements, while maintaining the ability to use negative bilateral incentives.

The negotiating team needs to be long-term and realistic, not changed after every election cycle, or bought off by employment blandishments from either China or the United States. China has the social and political structure to keep people focused on a long-term negotiation. Does the United States have the political will to negotiate in this way?

Notes

1. David Mitrany, *The Functional Theory of Politics*, London: London School of Economics and Political Science; New York: St. Martin's Press, 1975.

2. Huawei officials advised Iraq telecommunications to get their basic switching equipment and routers out of the exchanges before the 2003 attack. Many employees took equipment home or to alternative sub exchanges. This indicates that there is some level of disaster preparedness in Chinese telecom policy.

3. James McGregor, *China's Drive for 'Indigenous Innovation': A Web of Industrial Policies*, Washington, DC: US Chamber of Commerce, 2010.

"Stuxnet and Cyber Conflict: Framing the Long Wave View" by Chris Demchak[1]

STUXNET IS TO TRADITIONAL CONFLICTS what the machine gun was to modern massed militaries. The operational and strategic effects played out less when the machine gun was first used than when it was applied at increased scale in the 1905 Russo-Japanese War and in WWI. All the pieces were known, but it required someone to put them together in the battlefield demonstrations that propelled decades of strategies, organizing, and development of new technologies. Stuxnet's designers combined known but otherwise unlinked elements of hardware, code, and routine human tendencies. They buried the hunting worm in the complexity of linked large-scale socio-technical systems to both fool the target's operators and hide the originators' identities. When the carefully-crafted software and its effects were publicly revealed, the world recognized a watershed moment in which software now could officially be weaponized and delivered hidden while traveling to its target across the thousands of combined human-machine networks forming the global cyberspace substrate.

Stuxnet accelerated nascent "cybered conflict." Henceforth, all societally important conflicts will be cybered, with cyber playing a role at key points in determining the conflicts' outcomes. Just as the machine gun married the scale of fire in more modern technological systems to the scale of massed military organizations, Stuxnet's designers employed the deceptiveness and opaqueness of one of the highly complex socio-technical systems of cyberspace against itself. Now conflict has become cybered explicitly and publicly. The complexity and connectivity of large-scale socio-technical systems are henceforth to be pitted against other such systems through deceptive exploits by obscured actors without warnings or indicators.

Today, the gauntlet has been thrown down for practitioners and scholars of national security to integrate the lessons of both the rise of cyber conflict and the strategic responses to Stuxnet-like campaigns. Missing in the traditional approaches to conflict is a cognitive framing that will allow more systemic integration across the diverse and rapid conceptual, strategic, technological, and political developments of a globally digitized world. One major response to the machine gun nest was the modern tank, but when it was developed, it was viewed just as a mobile armored machine gun vehicle by its early innovators, the British. Today, one does not have twenty years to serendipitously discover a cyber conflict Guderian or MacArthur who can see how the long wave systemic trends will be further accelerated by the Stuxnet demonstration. Now the deadline for a better framing is on cyber time, with tens of thousands of individuals looking to what can be developed from what Stuxnet revealed for offense or defense in a multi-upon-multiplayer undeclared, deceptive, opaque conflict. The stakes are no less than salvaging what may be saved in the formerly open, unfettered, nearly free, ubiquitous, and generative cyberspace built with optimism, naiveté, and hubris by liberal democratic civil societies for largely economic reasons. Stuxnet demonstrated how normal routines of complex systems can be made deceptive, surprising, and exceptionally dangerous without a known opponent anywhere near the locus or range of effects.

This piece argues that one can build on the already available resilience and surprise research of the large-scale socio-technical systems (LTS) studies community. Its recommendations help to frame a long wave evolutionary vision including emergent Stuxnet-informed cyber conflict, the rising Cyber Westphalia, and beyond to resilience-seeking clustering of like-minded states. This piece extends into post-Stuxnet conflict and international system topological changes empirical LTS observations about what most people do when they fear systemic surprise and the subsequently systemic effects.

SURPRISE AND RESILIENCE IN LARGE-SCALE SOCIO-TECHNICAL SYSTEMS

The empirical question is: how should large-scale democratic socio-technical-economic systems underpinning modern societies best frame and implement a response to deliberate, accidental, and opportunistic surprise? Beyond international relations, security studies, and international economics, there are other disciplines that have dealt with complex systems forced into dysfunction by surprise or malevolence whose ideas can help in developing systemic national responses to cyber conflict.

One body of literature outside of the normal security studies/international relations world of particular relevance is that of large-scale socio-technical systems (LTS). For more than thirty-five years, the LTS community has been looking into how large complex systems involving humans can avoid the nasty surprises inherent in large-scale complexity, especially those that break apart critically important assemblages and hurt people. Using complexity theory and empirical research, the LTS community developed the first of two major framing recommendations. For singleton enterprises, militaries, or nations facing complex system surprises that are unknowable in form or frequency in advance, the best one can do is be continuously resilient. Systemic resilience means three requirements at a base organizational level: to be redundant in knowledge, to have slack time to accommodate surprises, and to continuously engage in discovery trial-and-error learning (DTEL) in order to make the first two effective.

The more unknowable in advance the possible surprises, the more critical it is to build in monitors and breaks, sometimes called "air gaps," throughout connected networks to slow the effects so responses can be initiated or developed on the spot. The more redundant the sources of knowledge in any form along the way, the more likely the rippling cascade effects of a surprise can be dampened by quickly-altered processes that keep operations functioning. A resilient system response to a Stuxnet-equivalent that damages process control systems, for example, would have to have many independent monitors and air gaps for slack, as well as multiple sources of responses when the centrifuges begin acting erratically, even though operating indicators of the malfunctioning process control command machines do not accurately reflect reality. Both responses would need to be frequently and routinely challenged, studied, and re-challenged to be prepared for surprise.

Beyond the singleton large-scale socio-technical enterprise, however, the LTS community's research offers a second set of resilience recommendations for the huge networks created when these single enterprises are linked together for efficiency reasons across regions and sectoral systems. Each linked enterprise needs its own resilience reinforced internally with the socialization and operationalization arising from being a single company or agency. The difficulty in a huge network is that these large-scale complex socio-technical systems are often made of independent strangers and sometimes competitors. Because the new networks are not bound by a single organization, they usually do not feel responsible for each other in the way members of an organization are socialized to accept. In a tightly-coupled large network, one organization can act for itself in seeking resilience, and in so doing, take down the wider system if the tightly-coupled others are not so resilient, a process now called globalization. This outcome is also possible if members of tightening networks do not know operationally what is best for their own or the wider network's well-being. Members of these more-tightly-coupled networks also might not necessarily be open to coordinating as one would expect in a single enterprise, even if they did not know what to do or were choosing the patently harmful choice. The LTS research suggests an additional two requirements beyond redundancy, slack, and DTEL to ensure critically linked socio-technical systems can compensate: developing shared knowledge and trust through frequently-practiced collective sense-making before and throughout any emergency; and through rapid, collective, well-tested, mitigating, and innovative reactions. These systems need to innovate in creating the next set of reactions to include a library of accessible possible alternative operations across a range of possible teams embedded in connected systems who nonetheless know each other and are familiar with their respective roles, systems, and limitations or special abilities.

In the same way, other fields of study, from psychology to sociology to resilience engineering, have come up with at least two of the same recommendations as LTS studies. Roughly stated, to be relatively safe from catastrophic surprise in complex systems, one should have enough information in advance (here labeled foreknowledge) collectively and continuously vetted, and be prepared to act rapidly, proactively, and innovatively as well as remedially. Militaries, particularly democratic professional services, have known both of these requirements for hundreds of years, although they have not always implemented them well. They expect to be surprised in battle and incorporate this expectation into technological preparations for possible future wars. Other enterprises that may link up with them in battle or as allies are not likely to be socialized or operationalized in compatible ways. So with militaries, the collection of foreknowledge about other organizations and the peacetime testing of possible joint operations are crucial tasks in defending against complex socio-technical systems surprise.

Stuxnet publicly confirmed the arrival of the cyber conflict era. Just as the "information age" was heralded in the 1990s as making everything digital into a source of knowledge and benefits, cyberspace carrying Stuxnets is now discussed as a source of weaponizable and systemic threats. By linking societies just as regional sectoral systems link single domestic firms, but without any consensual socialization or legitimated operationalization, the unfettered global digital cyberspace substrate by its opaqueness and complexity allows the use of the same tools for generative productivity as it does for harm and nasty surprises. Three traditional systemic hindrances to offense and predatory behaviors built largely on geographic separations and lags in response times have correspondingly dramatically declined with the diminution of distance and time offered by today's web. The scale of resources required for organizing armies, ensuring proximity for intelligence-gathering, and developing precision technology to reliably overmatch targets were throughout history very expensive and time-consuming, and as a result remained the exclusive province of empires or super-powers. Now anyone can participate in organizing five to five thousand attackers, in gathering high-quality intelligence without close proximity to any targets, and in targeting with great precision cities, individuals, and firms all at the same time. The result has been twenty years of increasingly free-for-all predation, and increasingly productive offense for a wide variety of state and nonstate actors.

Stuxnet's designers raised the tools of cybercrime to the next level through development of systemic offense advantages. The obscured originators of Stuxnet demonstrated a command of cyberspace's scale, proximity, and precision benefits by carefully designing a tool meant for one target while delivering it via the mass offense-friendly cyberspace substrate. With Stuxnet, deception and opaqueness became critical attributes of cyber conflict in a way they had never been since the advent of mass armies, massed mechanized forces, and even nuclear weapons. Stuxnet used the tools of the technological system exactly as they were intended to be used, but by careful distortion, managed the effects its designers desired while remaining unknown to its distant target. Stuxnet demonstrated that it is possible to take any mechanized and digitally connected and controlled item that needs electricity and has flammable or other properties able to cause harm, and remotely and deceptively manipulate that item to disable it or potentially harm others singly, en masse, or in selective groups. Stuxnet showed that predatory cyber tools need not accomplish this manipulation directly, but can be sent out into the wild of the global web, floating benignly through innocent hosts with the intent of harming one or more targets, all at once or over time, in small and continuing ways or one big flash, at the designers' will. The delivery of Stuxnet demonstrated that being geographically disconnected or distant is no protection as long as any element of the relevant socio-technical-economic systems is accessible, unmonitored, and not resilient to even barely skilled, deceptive, opaque, hostile, or opportunistic attackers.

Post-Stuxnet and its peers, cyber conflict is now more clearly composed of struggles between systems in which everything is potentially dual-use, from rather basic machine controllers to printers on networks. What is and is not a weapon has been thrust back five centuries to when the weapons people used for war were the tools they used for hunting and in the fields. Just like plague-infected blankets traded innocently and not-so-innocently three hundred years ago, one can receive malware-infected computers right out of their manufacturing boxes. These basic systems can be so infected and so willing to work for distant masters that they must simply be trashed after the infection is revealed. One has also learned that there are massive numbers of groups, individuals, and now states willing to spend years and years finding unmonitored, untraceable, and unpunishable access points through which to pursue their particular agendas in harm.

Stuxnet's designers cleverly used humans to move across what should have been gaps in connections between critical systems. Now each confident, productive, democratic civil society must spend a good part of its future basically protecting itself from everything that is shared or developed remotely and in any way digitized. One can no longer safely and casually design socio-technical-economic systems as if connected, digitized products are like cars that can be turned on and will run reliably for the life of the machine with modest care. In the cyber conflict era, anything that comes from afar and cannot be independently tested and, if infected, returned to the originator via punishment, is a potential threat that someone will eventually attempt to exploit.

One analogy may be that modern societies today may need to treat everything that is remotely digitally connected or created much as early industrializing nations once had to treat food that came from anywhere outside of the local community. Corrupted food sometimes smells bad, but often lethal food-borne threats are not discernible by any of the routine senses. Many sources of fluid contamination do not manifest immediate effects. Systemic harm historically has come more by accident then by deliberate intent, but the effect on societies has been catastrophic over time. Take, for example, lead in the ubiquitous pipes used by the Romans for their heating and their water, and in the pottery off which they ate. The Romans considered their aqueducts and piping into homes as markers of their advanced civilization, but the hidden threats in those critical systems nonetheless literally killed them.

Democratic civil societies generally develop institutional responses to society-wide threats so as to have the resources to develop necessary knowledge and legal authorities to enforce principles or sanctions to punish predators and deter opportunists. Industrialized, domestic food supplies again are good examples of this process. In each democratic civil society, there are agencies whose purpose is to check food and to punish those who market or deliver bad food from outside a local community. National context enables this response because of the overarching society's monopoly of force and legitimacy. The food producers are not connected organizationally to each consumer, and thus they have no common socialization or operationalization incentives. The wider political system, however, compensates with its sources of authority (socialization) and regulations (operationalization) to force food producers to act as though they are in a collective and organized entity with consumers, creating shared responsibility for the resilience of food supply systems. In this way, societies' political leaders can force slack time to respond to food shortages, redundancy of knowledge in developing alternative food supplies, and also discovery trial-and-error learning about how to maintain food supplies for national food resilience against urgent surprises disrupting systemic conditions.

However, and importantly for this discussion, a source of threat beyond the home society's monopoly of force often induces the imposition of barriers to entry because few other resilience levers exist. When the producers of routinely bad food were not under a given society's monopoly of force, nations often enough banned the import of that food. If the government did not, individuals learned to avoid that food or that producer of routinely bad food. A good example of this is the current shortage of baby formula in China after the discovery that baby formula sold by domestic producers in China was laced with a toxic whitening substance that killed infants.

In a similar fashion, the threat-carrying capacity of the global cyberspace substrate is already inducing barriers against threats emerging from beyond a nation's geographic borders. The lessons of the LTS community, especially the need for slack time for systemic resilience, apply to surprises across the complex systems of cyberspace, particularly when the sources of surprise are inalterably large-scale, multisourced, and undeterrable in the main by proactive, individually-targeted actions.

Resilience under those circumstances tends to be difficult and often not affordable for a single enterprise trying to meet all of the LTS requirements. History suggests that such threats have usually been addressed by the least costly of the three original resilience requirements. Slack time is usually attempted first and is found throughout history in various forms from gates and city walls to watch towers and forward forces to armed national borders with military forces behind them. The efforts attempt to push the sources of nasty systemic surprises as far away in time, which usually meant geography, as possible for as long a period as possible. Organizations in states deeply embedded in globalization are beginning to individually withdraw in bits and pieces behind clouds, firewalls, encryption, and new punitive rules for predatory behavior enforced by the overarching society's monopoly of force.

RISING CYBER WESTPHALIA

Today, as a result, the institutional and technological building blocks of national virtual borders are rising across cyberspace, a trend Stuxnet helped accelerate. State leaders are in particular looking to making the largely nationally-regulated telecommunications firms of each society into the central building blocks of the national scheme for cleansing malicious software from the cyber networks of modern democracies. If current trends hold, and there is every reason to believe they will, eventually a "Cyber Westphalia" of national jurisdictions parsing the global web will emerge. The goal of these eventual virtual borders is to reduce the overwhelming volume of harmful surprises, especially economically-related, accumulating from the massive and relentless efforts by hundreds of thousands of bad actors reaching through the globally-shared cyberspace substrate to exploit distant strangers. The scale and nonstop pace of this flood of malicious attempts outweighs the sophistication and skill of most of these bad actors so that they collectively create discernible patterns over time. Since many physical or normal elements of our lives now have a dual-use capacity which can possibly be subverted to harm without any alert or change in performance, borders constitute efforts to introduce slack time by reducing the overwhelming input even at lower levels of skill. In principle, it is possible for these national virtual responses to be designed to stall, cleanse, track, or perhaps automatically strike back punitively when such patterns of attack are detected. In addition, national standards can be used internally to require national domestically-operated networks to be less vulnerable socio-technically to these patterns or to create preferable positive transformations of the underlying layer of cyber technologies.

Such borders, if well-designed and continuously innovative, do contribute to overall national resilience to the transformations. Properly curtailing the ease with which malicious software can be transmitted, they can reduce to a large extent the three easy offensive advantages enjoyed by most remote and opaque bad actors, whether skilled or not: scale in organizing, proximity for intelligence, and wide choices in targeting precision. The reduced flow of "noise" is therefore also less available for future Stuxnet-like worm designers to use as convenient camouflage through which to disperse their hunting worms toward the target without revealing themselves. The delivery design of Stuxnet reinforced the obvious point that the globally massive scales of complex transactions across the cyberspace substrate were operationally useful for offense but a liability for defense. Malware could be deceptively and opaquely designed to carry malicious surprises through a very large number of host carriers without harming them and yet find and harm specific targets. One could even call this "computer DNA swarming." Stuxnet showed that malware can find the targeted needle in a haystack even when the specific human targets do not realize they are being hunted and their critical technological nodes are considered offline.

Stuxnet's design, execution, and effects reinforce the distinctiveness of cyber conflict as state-to-state campaigns remotely, deceptively, and opaquely using surprise against a targeted nation's systems without declaring hostilities. This new form of conflict is social, technical, and economic in reach without being easily discernible in progress or publicly owned by any of the participating sides. Stuxnet established what can be done across the noise of global cyberspace if the hunter knows the target's socio-technical architecture including technology variants, processes, operational presumptions, authority structures, observed legal restraints, and routine or critical uses, including such exploitable tools as USB sticks and network printers. If the decline of the open, unfettered, and yet safe cyberspace was not self-evident before Stuxnet was revealed, it certainly is now clear in the post-Stuxnet period. Stuxnet demonstrated that one cannot presume everyone with access to one's own systems means to use them in the way the original designers innocently intended.

National virtual borders, however well they provide some slack time for states, do not provide the redundancy in knowledge or the continuous feedback for innovation in discovery trial-and-error learning required for any nation to be fully resilient unto itself. In this new world of not being able to trust any product that has been digitized along its production delivery and use chain, democratic civil societies must alter the domestic circumstances that support the three cyberspace offensive advantages in slack, proximity, and precision. Borders change proximity the most directly. Cyberspace is entirely human-made, owned, maintained, operated, and adapted. In principle, democratic civil societies can force its transformation to be more systemically resilient in architecture, but only in the parts they eventually jurisdictionally and individually control. Stuxnet's revelation made it clear that competition and conflict between peoples from here on will be systems against systems wherever they critically connect, be that within, on, or across national jurisdictions.

LONG WAVE OPTIMISM: RISE OF MUTUALLY SECURED RESILIENCE

Virtual borders are now inevitable in this rising future Cyber Westphalia, but for the resilience of any nation, they will never be sufficient.

Even as the floods are reduced and what is allowed transit through the links of the cyberspace substrate becomes more regularized, global complexity will remain high within and among nations. The disadvantage for individual democratic civil society defenders is that the highly insecure cyberspace substrate is now ubiquitous throughout and across societies that are currently no longer able to autarkically and individually function economically without the flows of transactions and goods across territorial borders. Plus, the nodes composing the socio-technical systems of the substrate are ever-multiplying in numbers and forms in terms of mobile devices and alternative sources for information that historically was never shared widely. Just like a single enterprise, modern democratic civil societies cannot close themselves off from their major economic peers to stop the massive bad actor noise or the future Stuxnets hidden in the floods.

Borders will rise, but, much like the networked enterprises studied in the LTS community's literature, individual nations will also inevitably discover that their attempts to maintain resilience and minimize disruption are becoming exhausting and insufficient as long as they are networked externally for critical goods and services. Furthermore, these societies will discover that their cyber commands cannot easily discern all the future Stuxnet or peer variants. Even if the noise of unskilled bad actors across cyberspace is reduced in externally-originating flows by national virtual borders, skilled adversaries will bypass defenses meant for the masses of unskilled actors. Forward disruption capacities are necessary, along with systemic national resilience, in order for nations to be robust cyber powers in this coming future; however, skilled designers and operators of future Stuxnets will continue to travel wherever those networks connect across states.

Unfortunately for these defenders, it is unlikely that international institutions can force compliance across the global substrate. Many discussions about international norms in cyberspace have come up short on actual implementation. There is no shared international "society" or sector able to use authority, incentives, and regulations to design, induce, and enforce collective resilience activities across nations as societies do across domestic networked critical systems.

At the end of the day, states will have to look to their regional or allied peers, much like enterprises within a single society must collectively create their own resilience across shared operational networks. The shared daily practices and cultural presumptions across cooperating states strongly influence the extent to which interstate agreements can serve the same purpose as an overarching society in orchestrating national network compliance among independent organizations that do not individually share the same socialization or operationalization incentives. European-derived societies built and enforced the liberal international system according to their preferences in order to reduce the costly surprises imposed on their economies by other cultures and the demands of distance. This historically-linked community of nations does have common shared cultural basics along with their contemporary transactions across socio-technical-economic systems. The wider global community of nations does not have these advantages. The reasons are the same as for any organization or sectoral association attempting to collectively organize resilience: if one does not share the same culture, socialization is very difficult. If there is any question about what must be done, and it coincides with a lack of socialization, cooperative operationalization is very difficult. Without either, it is exceptionally hard across all nations and cultures to create the authority and coordination incentives needed for collective resilience across the entire world connected to cyberspace. At the very least, attempting to make the whole world cooperate as one organization might for collective resilience is not empirically shown to be a reasonable first step in securing cyberspace. Conversely, among the regional nations of Europe and the Americas, there is the possibility of enacting the second set of LTS recommendations for collective resilience against complex socio-technical systems surprise across linked states and their enterprises.

Furthermore, these shared culture and operational histories facilitate systemic resilience cooperation from the private but critical sectors of democratic civil societies. Private enterprises are key players in controlling cyber access across national borders today, and they will continue to be in the future cyber-bordered world. Therefore, the choices made by private sector leaders will play a singularly important role in making the domestic cyberspace substrate of each state resilient or vulnerable in the future. The private sectors of Europe and the Americas have deep roots in cooperating and competing under broadly similar rules of the road. They are among the largest losers of the victims of cybercrime, and, in recent research, their private sector losses are now shown to cumulate in debilitating decreases in national GDP growth rates. They cannot operate alone any more than any single enterprise could operate alone to protect itself alone against complex systems surprise while connected to other enterprises. Their willingness to collectively develop sense-making and innovative rapid reactions will be essential for national resilience as well, and it is more likely to be obtainable among the subset of states whose private enterprises also share well-established cultural and operational relations.

Over the long run, if the democratic civil societies of Europe and the Americas are to find the cyber resilience they need and yet preserve the free, open cyberspace they optimistically built, they will need to work together as they require their own domestic, digitized socio-technical systems in a shared critical sector to do already. In moving to make their own domestically-protected substrates, modern democratic civil societies cannot individually make the whole world comply with innocuous uses of the Internet as it was originally designed. They will shortly or already no longer have the political, military, or economic clout to force the other 80 percent of the world's population to restrain exploitation of whatever remains of the unfettered global web and of the liberal international system Europeans constructed over the past two hundred years. If these civil societies intend to continue as systems linked to the wider cyber international system, they can ultimately only protect themselves from malicious and cascading complex systems surprises when they join together with like-minded civil societies to collectively create resilience.

Furthermore, if there is to be an Internet that is free and still safe to use widely in some part of the globe, it will have to be among these democratic nations creating a liberal and resilient post-Cyber Westphalian system secured on a regional scale. These particular civil societies have available the socialization advantages of being like-minded cultures and the operationalization advantages of having been the original designers of the ubiquitous Internet and now long-term deeply entrenched economic partners. There will need to be a shared vision of "mutually secured resilience" against both the masses of bad actors and the smaller sets of highly-skilled actors behind future Stuxnet-like operations developed across these societies. Those threats undeterrable by virtual borders require not just resilience but also mutually-controlled forward disruptive capacities operating externally to this regional collective. This regionally-resilient cyberspace can then form an alternative to the way cyberspace is likely to develop given the current anti-liberal and highly predatory trends. If very little changes in terms of the systemic offensive advantages of cyberspace, the formerly unfettered digital global substrate is likely to be both increasingly fragmented and controlled by governments in functional states, as well as widely compromised by exploitations from organizations and individuals in semi-functional parts of the world.

CONCLUSION

This vision of the long wave evolutionary path of the global cyberspace substrate is not the optimistic vision of the cyber prophets in the 1990s, nor is it the devastating apocalyptic vision that many of those same people have today about the rise of a cyber world of national jurisdictions. Rather, it is a world adjusting to the deception and opaqueness that came with the global opening of rule of law societies to others that never shared, and could not be forced to observe, the democratic civil society constraints or laws assumed to function everywhere by the somewhat naïve originators of the global Internet. Stuxnet did not change the trajectory of cyber conflict so much as it highlighted and illuminated the kind of highly deceptive and opaque conflicts that this currently unfettered, near-free, and ubiquitous cyberspace substrate can readily produce. Stuxnet induced across many public and private leaders watershed feelings of surprise that tend to propel them to action and thus accelerate wider trends.

Furthermore, in terms of the long wave evolution of cyberspace, it does not really matter which state or states designed and released

Stuxnet. It is now a fact open to all to pursue systemically across the cyberspace substrate. The machine gun did not vanish as a defeated and irrelevant tool of compellence. Rather, it evolved to its portable offspring, the high-firepower assault rifle, which individuals acquire from arms dealers across borders in floods and then use to challenge and destabilize state monopolies of power and institutional effectiveness from within. Only in those nations able to assert their prerogatives both at the border and within are these easily portable and securable machines not posing existential threats to national functions.

That is, these states controlled such weapons up to now, before the full onslaught of the highly-sophisticated, locally-controlled, monitored, and obscured 3D printing machine makes it possible to individually and affordably produce weapons able to fire relatively accurately more than once. Easy, cheap, and ubiquitous reproducibility of knowledge in the form of dual-use technologies not easily controlled by the existing state's monopoly of force is a large part of the much-lauded "information age" that was optimistically promised. The early cyber prophets naïvely neglected what dual-use could actually mean for the stability and well-being of large-scale, highly-integrated societies.

Today, no one state is particularly privileged as a robust cyber power with the resilience and disruptive capacities to fire and absorb Stuxnet-like hits at high pace and volume, and at will. There are no guarantees about which cultures and nations will dominate the future digitally-connected globe and the socio-technical-economic surprises that are delivered. In this context, and before it is too late politically or financially, if the designers of the Internet seek to save what they originally intended to offer the world, and their own socio-technical-economic systems in the bargain, they need to hang together in cyberspace. If not, as trends are, they most certainly will hang separately and become declining powers in the future world.

Notes

1.   The "Cyber Westphalia" concept was jointly developed in collaboration with Peter J. Dombrowski in Chris C. Demchak and Peter J. Dombrowski, "Rise of a Cybered Westphalian Age," *Strategic Studies Quarterly* 5, no. 1 (2011): 31-62. His contribution must be acknowledged here as well as continuing long wave work in this area.

"A Stuxnetted Future"
by Michael Schrage

SEPTEMBER 11, 2021, IS A day that will live in infamy forever. At 7:07 a.m. sharp, subway cars in Boston, New York, and Washington, DC, were wracked by literally hundreds of explosions. Many had the percussive force of small firecrackers before bursting into flame. But most were more powerful than M-80s. Fingers and faces were seared and torn off.

The next round of explosions came seventy-seven seconds later. Hundreds were severely burnt and blinded. Thousands more were trampled as panicked commuters struggled to escape the smoke-filled trains. The subway stations were similarly devastated; the bloody platforms look like war zones. Because they were.

The story was no better above ground. All along America's East Coast, rush hour trucks and automobiles on freeways, highways, and city streets spun out of control as synchronized explosions crippled drivers. Major thoroughfares quickly became smoking ruins. More than a score of "standing room only" packed New York City and Philadelphia buses ignited into blazing infernos. Nearly everyone on board them was killed. High school and junior high buses across the Northeast were similarly hit. Practically all surviving children suffered third-degree burns to their faces and hands.

Exactly one hour later, similar urban, suburban, and automotive destruction occurred throughout Chicago and the Midwest.

At 9:11 a.m., planes begin dropping out of the sky. Not all of them, but more than a dozen general aviation aircraft and regional jets. Virtually every commercial flight radioed "Mayday" because cockpit and cabin fires with terribly wounded passengers and pilots demanded action. Virtually every commercial flight in the air that morning requested immediate permission to land. However, scores of small explosions in the main terminals of JFK, LaGuardia, Newark, Logan, and O'Hare had forced evacuation of personnel and shutdowns.

Needless to say, the simultaneity and severity of the attacks produced tsunamis of emergency calls, texts, and emails. Regional and national telecom networks were overwhelmed. Alas, crude but modestly successful efforts to sabotage municipal cellphone towers and slice a couple of fiber-optic cables exacerbated the crises. Rumors soon swirled that the decapitated bodies of two Verizon and AT&T maintenance people had been found. YouTube and Vine videos were simultaneously posted in Abbottabad and London.

California and the West Coast were next.

What happened? Upon review, the essential malware was simple, ingenious, and scalably effective—a masterpiece of digital infiltration, espionage, and sabotage. The tightly-packed code basically turned every smartphone, tablet, and eyewear running Android, IOS, or Microsoft HoloLens operating systems into digital IEDS. Call them DIEDs.

The malware quietly but thoroughly corrupted device power management systems. When cued by time, geolocation, and/or accelerometer-ascertained speed, that malware turned batteries into bombs.

The bigger and denser the battery, the more destructive the resulting explosion and fire. Anyone with a device in their hands, on their laps, or pressing their cheeks would be wounded or worse. Phones affixed to automobile dashboards or tablets entertaining children were virtually guaranteed to inflict grievous harm.

The more networked devices one carried, the greater the opportunities for dismemberment and death. The multiplicative power of hundreds of such devices simultaneously erupting on city buses or subway cars virtually guaranteed death or dismemberment. That second explosive wave sealed in the initial terror and pain. Everyone trying to make emergency calls, texts, or tweets during that eerily silent seventy-seven-second gap had fingers and faces mutilated.

Weeks later, forensic analyses ultimately revealed fewer than 4.5 million infected devices—barely 3 percent of the accessible population—were enough wreak this havoc. Between porn sites, a handful of free Trojan horse apps, and skillfully-designed viral attachments, spreading the essential malware took fewer than fifty days. Cleverly concealed loggers tracked infected devices and users; the plotters fine-tuned and better targeted their explosive impact accordingly.

For all intents and purposes, moderately talented terrorists cost-effectively converted Botnet paradigms and templates into battlespaces that transformed people's personal devices into networked booby-traps. Their phones and tablets DIED to attack them.

Technically, this was the largest strategic bombing strike and local terror tactic in world history.

The attack killed more Americans than the jet-fueled collapse of the Twin Towers and the attack on the Pentagon. No last-minute "Let's Roll" heroics thwarted the lethality of literally millions of traveling IEDs.

Pointing out possible vulnerabilities in next-gen telecommunications networks is not the purpose of this wicked scenario; how "Stuxnetification" requires serious students of military conflict and technology to revisit and rethink fundamental assumptions about warfare is.

This brief essay asserts Stuxnet's perceived successes—and limitations—invite revision of nascent cyber conflict doctrines, net-centric warfare beliefs, C3I/ISR operations, and the future of combined arms. The goal is to provoke useful arguments between national security constituencies who are too often too quick to either compartmentalize novel technologies or pursue grand strategic CONOPS.

Ideally, those useful arguments will help military leaders, policymakers, and those who preserve, protect, and defend critical infrastructures better understand and manage the risks and opportunities tomorrow's Stuxnets will create.

For this essay, the most important Stuxnet insight is that networked computation becomes "intelligently kinetic." That is, malware should no longer be seen as simply about digitally crippling, killing, or stealthily parasitizing components of complex "dual use" systems. Malware can dimensionally re-engineer and transform those components—and thus that system—into something else.

This malware genre facilitates the creation of new capabilities that elicit novel effects. Stuxnet was a crudely important first step towards technically highlighting the false dichotomies and real interfaces between atoms and bits. Tomorrow's Stuxnets will be far more talented and versatile technical traitors. What is more, they will learn. Over time, we will see the Watsonification of Stuxnets. That is to say, machine-learning enabled malware that gets smarter when either opportunities or threats materialize.

Consequently, Stuxnetification blurs, if not smears, the boundaries between the virtual and physical, military and civilian, visual and acoustic, chemical and electrical, and between software, firmware, and hardware. Interoperability between networks and their nodes mutates from enabler to "schwachpunkt" vulnerability. Stuxnetification dramatically expands the degrees of freedom and control for an intruder. The more sweeping, pervasive, and empowering the interoperability, the more transformationally toxic next-gen Stuxnets can be.

In an era of autonomous cars, 3D printers, nanotech fabricators, home automation systems, and DIY drones, the opportunities for innovative mayhem combinatorially explode. Stuxnetified ensembles could literally induce apartment complexes—or entire neighborhoods—to set themselves aflame or seduce self-driving cars into precision-ferrying lethal weaponry. Stuxnets do not just enjoy such "target-rich" environments and ecosystems; they will create them.

These malware become less "force multiplier" than "effects enabler." Wherever "embedded intelligence" (in virtually any form) influences physical/kinetic outcomes (in virtually any form), ingeniously vicious—and viciously ingenious—warfighters will be spoilt for choice.

But identifying, appreciating, and acting upon those innovative choices will likely demand more than a technically-informed rereading of Clausewitz, Kahn, Schelling, and Lao Tzu. A serious deconstruction of Stuxnet suggests that its true socio-politico-military potential goes well beyond technological prowess. Future reality suggests Stuxnetification demands doctrinal re-evaluation of how national security institutions project force, prosecute wars, and protect populations.

This will be as true for peer-to-peer "superpower" conflicts as for COIN. (Consider this thought experiment: imagine Stuxnet-like malware that prevents mobile devices from being used as IED detonators while quietly uploading location and contents to the nearest "friendlies." What happens when popular and pervasive personal technologies are rendered useless as "IED enablers"?)

In these "super-Stuxnet scenarios," networks simultaneously become both battlefield and weapon. Note this cannot be accurately said of land, sea, air, or space...or bullets, bombs, drones, and ICBMs. They are either one or the other. Stuxnets make networks a weapon and weapons into networks. Stuxnets innovatively inaugurate a new "Age of –age"—espionage, camouflage, sabotage, barrage, and so on. Malware multivalence makes Stuxnets more than a virus or a worm; it transforms and transmutes. Malware evolves.

Stuxnetification's ongoing boundary-blurring inherently means one cannot be certain, for example, where the espionage ends and the sabotage begins, or vice versa. (This was the thesis of the *Financial Times* "Comment" that inspired this essay.) Or where camouflage ends and a barrage begins.

Consider, for example, a "super-Stux" infecting a petrochemical refinery. Every five hundredth batch of fuel oil is usefully and trackably tainted. As the facility attempts to up-tempo its operations and productivity to support a hostile actor, every three hundredth batch is trackably tainted...then every hundredth. Espionage, sabotage, and infiltrational tempo are inextricably linked.

Extend that intelligent corruption-disruption model to traffic networks, telecom networks, pipelines, and power grids—anything that might reasonably be defined as critical infrastructure. Stuxnetification's transformational paradigm invites unusual and asymmetric answers to both strategic and tactical warfighting questions.

After all, the ability to selectively squeeze a system—with the omnipresent option to crush it at will—is enormously powerful. The more traditional kinetic military option to shut down or destroy outright remains. But the creatively competent warfighter and/or political overseer wonders what is the smarter and more strategic exercise. What effect—or combination of effects—gives better politico-military value? What happens to morale and materiel as complex systems are induced to overtly and/or covertly betray their masters? If we take Liddell Hart's famous quote, "To influence man's thought is far more important and more lasting in effect than to control their bodies or regulate their actions" seriously, then Stuxnetification makes these questions less rhetorical than operational.[1]

For example, who in the chain of command steps up as the "Stuxnet squeeze" intensifies? Which leaders emerge? What logistical backups are revealed and/or employed? Stuxnetification does not just permit, it provokes both the creation and calibration of new targeting opportunities for interdiction, intervention, co-option, assassination, and/or elimination. Do warfighters get more value from espionage or sabotage? Do we gain greater tactical insights from disruption or destruction? Strategic Stuxnetification creates new tradespaces for tacticians and master strategists alike.

For example, randomly or selectively disrupting an urban cellular telecom network might generate more useful and usable intelligence than completely suppressing it. Might Stuxnetifying cellphone towers and Wi-Fi hotspots yield not just rich harvests of analytic intelligence but sow useful doubts about what telecom contingency plans to employ? Some phones hiss and crackle, others garble texts and emails; some work intermittently, others work perfectly, and several go dead for hours at a time. These become data, not just effects.

Stuxnetification generates structured uncertainties that undermine reliability and confidence. Just as fears of a misfiring weapon makes soldiers hesitate to charge, malfunctioning or deteriorating support systems sap resolve. *Knowing* something does not work is certainty; rationally *doubting* how well critical technologies might perform under fire creates fear.

Imagine emotional contagions as mobile devices explode in people's faces or cars mysteriously accelerate themselves into walls.

Stuxnetification post-industrially deters, dissuades, disrupts, and destroys technical trust. Subverting trust is an effect both a Lao Tzu and Clausewitz would appreciate.

Do we more effectively impose our will by the explicit targeting effects or via less discriminating interventions? Innovative Stuxnetification could facilitate the innovative identification and segmentation of more hostile or potentially acquiescent populations. Again, observing populations and their responses to effects generates better and more actionable intelligence. In twenty-first century warfare, SDA—Stuxnetification Damage Assessments—will likely prove far more valuable to tomorrow's warfighters than Bomb Damage Assessments.

But extracting meaningful situational awareness requires more than superior military expertise or more sophisticated COIN advisors. Strategists, tacticians, and policymakers alike will be pushed to consider novel doctrines of dissuasion, deterrence, disruption, and destruction.

With apologies to the microeconomists, Stuxnetification's tunable network effects should not be viewed independently or in isolation. They are intrinsically different from, say, firepower or electronic warfare.

In practice, they should enable and empower new genres of "combined arms" that— potentially—are as strategically, organizationally, and operationally profound as radar's impact on fighter command, Pete Queseda's "close air support," or the pervasive rise of battlespace GPS.

The critical difference? Stuxnetification is explicitly designed to create technical traitors and virtual Fifth Columns within adversary infrastructures and their associated devices. The ability to internally corrupt and deceive may be more powerful than the capability to disrupt and destroy.

For example, might "smart additives" in gasoline blow up internal combustion engines after the third, fourth, or fifth time the vehicle traveled faster than 50 kmph for more than five minutes? How might purification plants be induced to pipe potable water that was "safe" to drink but tasted horrible and/or made boiling dangerous? What devices could be added to power grids that could stealthily monitor and short out industrial equipment?

Stuxnetification expands the operational bandwidth not just for shaping the battlespace, but extending the battlespace into hitherto unimagined domains. That is achieved by the decision to make adversaries—and the populations supporting them—wary, hesitant, and fearful about using the technologies and critical infrastructures that support their everyday lives. Is that a form of collective punishment or terrorism? Or does, in reality, that versatility make human conflict more humane?

Ideally, Stuxnetification is as much an attack on an enemy's will and morale as their technical capabilities and competences. Much the way that suppressive fire will not kill hostiles but precludes their ability to accurately target, a Stuxnet disruption undermines the willingness and ability of adversaries to respond to more direct forms of kinetic confrontation.

As the Sony episode emphatically illustrates, there is legal, political, and even military confusion as to whether cyberattacks should be interpreted as cyber vandalism or acts of war. The boundary-blurring themes highlighted here assure that JAGs, diplomats, and lawyers worldwide will have multiple opportunities to debate which legal regimes are most appropriate for a Stuxnetified world.

But just as war is too important to be left to the generals, Stuxnetification is too important to be left to the hackers and their legal advisers. The reality is that Stuxnets and Stuxnetification—like ancient swords—cruelly cut both ways. Our networked vulnerabilities are their opportunities, and vice versa. Serious policymakers and military leaders need the courage and insight to recognize that a few lines of code can turn a smartphone into a smart bomb.

Will that require a new level of military-civilian cooperation and oversight? Yes. Right now. Stuxnet may not be the harbinger of an existential threat but it is—emphatically—the next generation armament that forever dissolves the boundaries between benign technology and lethal weapon.

Notes

1.   B.H. Liddell Hart, "Thoughts on Philosophy, Politics, and Military Matters," June 7, 1932, Liddell Hart Papers II/1932/20.

Index

A

Ahmadinejad, President Mahmoud 3, 7
Alexander, General Keith 26
Alimohammadi, Masoud 8
American Chamber of Commerce in China 147
Ashkenazi, Lieutenant General Gabi 9, 20
Association of Southeast Asian Nations 18
Atlantic Council 22
Austin, Greg 100, 104

B

Baer, Merritt vii, 13, 29, 30, 83, 93
Baker, Chief Judge Jamie 87
Barzashka, Ivanka 8
Basij 25
Begin Doctrine 7
BRICS 98, 116
Budapest Conference on Cybercrime 117
bunker-busting bombs 4
Bushehr nuclear facility 112, 119, 120, 135
Bush, President George W. 4, 6, 7, 9, 14, 75
  Bush administration 4, 6, 7, 9, 75

C

Caroline affair 75
Cartwright, Vice Chairman of the Joint Chiefs of Staff General James 9
Cavelty, Myriam Dunn 101
Center for Political Studies 118
Center for Strategic and International Studies 95
Center for Technology and National Security Policy 143
Chen Fusheng 125
Chernobyl disaster 112
Chevron 4, 90

CPSIA information can be obtained
at www.ICGtesting.com
Printed in the USA
FFOW04n0906060616
24682FF